LEARNING C with tiny C

To the Bear and the Muffin

LEARNING C with tiny C

Scott B. Guthery

TAB BOOKS Inc.
Blue Ridge Summit, PA 17214

tiny-c® is a registered trademark of Scott B. Guthery and Thomas A. Gibson.
PDP-11™ is a trademark of Digital Equipment Corporation.
IBM PC® and PCjr® are registered trademarks of International Business Machines Corporation.
Unix™ is a trademark of AT&T Technology.

FIRST EDITION

FIRST PRINTING

Printed in the United States of America

Library of Congress Cataloging in Publication Data

Guthery, Scott B.
Learning C with tiny-c.

Includes index.
1. C (Computer program language) 2. Small-C
(Computer program language) I. Title.
QA76.73.C15G98 1985 001.64'24 85-4668
ISBN 0-8306-1895-3 (pbk.)

Contents

Preface

The tiny-c language was written originally by Tom Gibson. Finding himself much more productive using C on his Unix system at work than he was using 8080 assembly language on his CP/M system at home, Tom wrote an interpreter in C for a very limited subset of the C language, which he then hand-translated into 8080 assembler. I worked with Tom at the time and was suffering a similar frustration—except my home computer was a PDP-11. There were no non-Unix C compilers generally available and I just couldn't find an extra $42,000 in the family budget for a Unix license, so I hand-translated the interpreter into PDP-11 assembler.

We discovered that other people wanted to have—and were even willing to pay for—copies of these programs. So we gave the language a name, tiny-c, made the program more portable and user-customizable, wrote documentation called *The tiny-c Owner's Manual,* and started selling the whole package for $100. *Learning C with tiny-c* is a reimplementation of tiny-c specifically for the IBM PC and PCjr.

The sources of ideas that went into tiny-c are many. First there is BASIC (Kemeny and Kurtz; 1967), which has become the *de facto* standard training language in the United States. It is popular in high schools, universities, and even in industry, where it is used for some production work.

Although BASIC has its faults, its one big strength is that it is easy to learn. This is largely because it offers a single computing environment. You do not have to remember the environment you are in, i.e., whether you are in edit mode, compile mode, link mode, system mode, run mode, etc., when giving a command. You can enter new program lines, change old ones, and start a program running, all from one command environment. There are no commands to shift from mode to mode. There are no relocatable object modules, link editors, and all the other paraphernalia of "real" computing. It is very simple and very adequate. Thus a focus is made on the essential elements of computing, as opposed to the elements of "wrestling" with a computer.

The Logo language (Feurzeig; 1975) is in many ways similar to tiny-c. It offers a structured language based on BASIC, as well as a single environment for programming and execution. Logo was used experimentally in public schools with very young children. The experiment showed that children could grasp simple computer concepts, work through a prepared set of exercises, and then do creative work of their own.

C (Ritchie, Kernighan, and Lesk; 1975) is a computer language designed by Dennis Ritchie of Bell Telephone Laboratories. C, from which tiny-c borrows its overall structure, is broadly used in universities and in industry. It has been used to program a very advanced and powerful computer operating system called Unix (Ritchie and Thompson; 1974). And yet it is a very simple language. C has no native input/output, e.g., read or print statements. Input/output is done using functions. Thus C concentrates on computing facilities, and allows external development or elaborations of input/output. This idea has been adopted for tiny-c.

The command environment for tiny-c is written in tiny-c. It needs no translation to the microprocessor's machine language. This corresponds somewhat to the idea of using C as the programming language to implement Unix. Although intended as a training aid for structured programming, tiny-c is no less a powerful language in its own right.

C has gained considerably in popularity over the last 5 years. Currently there are high-quality compilers available on almost every machine and operating system, including many for the IBM PC and PCjr. Thus, even though the original reason for tiny-c's existence has passed into history, I believe it still has two contributions to make.

First, tiny-c is an easy-to-reach stepping stone from the monolithic world of BASIC programming to the highly modularized world of structured programming. While BASIC does a good job of teaching the fundamentals of computing, it does not do a good job of teaching program design. Structured programming has been developed to address problems of program design, and tiny-c is a beginner's structured programming language.

Second, since tiny-c is so small, the entire system is easily understood and easily modified to suit individual tastes. I like to think of tiny-c as a useful piece of laboratory equipment in a beginner's course in computer languages. You can study it, you can take it apart, you can change it, and you can put it back together without much trouble at all.

Soon, of course, you will want to get on to bigger and more challenging ventures. But if tiny-c can convince you that interpreters, compilers, and operating systems aren't magical black boxes but are programs that shuffle their bytes just like any other, then it will have earned its keep by opening for you the door to another exciting part of computer science.

Foreword

C is a versatile, expressive general-purpose programming language which offers economy of expression, modern control flow and data structures, and a rich set of operators. C is not a "very high-level" language, nor a "big" one, nor is it specialized to any particular area of application. But its absence of restrictions and its generality make it remarkably convenient and effective for a wide variety of computing tasks.

C is concise—you don't have to write a lot to get a job done. Yet at the same time, C programs are readable—you can understand what has been written. This combination of brevity and readability is rare in programming languages, and is part of the reason that C is so widely used.

With tiny-c, Tom Gibson and Scott Guthery have designed a stripped-down version of C that is well adapted to the microcomputer environment. The tiny-c language retains C's expressiveness, conciseness, and readability, yet sacrifices very few of its features.

At the same time, tiny-c provides a computing environment that will make it easier to develop programs. It comes with an editor and other piece parts that together make a program preparation system.

This book is more than a reference manual for tiny-c, however. It is also a vehicle for conveying ideas and insights about how to get the most out of your machine, and about good programming in general.

C has simply taken over in many computing environments, not because people have been ordered to use it, but because it is a good language. It seems very likely that tiny-c will have a similar effect in the microcomputer world.

BRIAN W. KERNIGHAN

LEARNING C with tiny C

Introduction

This book is about the tiny-c programming language. It's going to teach you everything—and I do mean *everything*—there is to know about tiny-c. First you'll learn how to use the system that lets you prepare and run tiny-c programs. Then you'll learn all about the tiny-c language. At this point you'll be able to write, debug, and run computer programs written in the tiny-c language, and build computer systems based on these programs.

This is about as far as most programming languages take you. Indeed, most of them feel that is as far as there is to go. But we're going to take a couple steps beyond. We're going to learn about the *insides* of the tiny-c programming system and about the *insides* of the tiny-c language processor.

An expert craftsman not only knows how to use his tools, but he also knows how his tools work. He uses this knowledge to personalize the tool so he can get that extra margin of high-precision performance that separates true craftsmanship from apprentice work. And so it should be with computer programs. Not just language programs but all programs. If you can't climb inside a program, tear it apart, tailor it, and put it back together so it fits you just right, then you don't really control it; it controls you.

We'll give you everything you need to take tiny-c apart and put it back together. It's up to you to make it your own.

PREREQUISITES AND GOALS

Programming is the biggest Adventure game ever. There are no physical laws to constrain the reality conjured into being by a programmer. You probably learned this first as a wanderer in other people's programs. Later you noticed it when you were doing the programming yourself. Every program is a dungeon populated by rewards, surprises, and beasts of every ilk. Some were put there deliberately by the programmer and some just invited themselves in.

As I begin to tell you about a new quest called "tiny-c," there are a few pieces of lore that I will assume you have already picked up in your peregrinations in the caves of computing.

I assume you know how to operate your computer: how to turn it on, how to use its operating system commands, how to create and edit a file, and how to load and run a program. If I tell you to load the tiny-c disk and start the **tinyc** program, I assume you know exactly what I mean and how to comply. I assume you know about the DOS commands and what files and directories are. If this is not true, I suggest you read the *IBM Guide to Operations* supplied with your computer.

Next, I assume you know something about programming. I assume you know what a program is, what a programming language is, and what it means to write, run, and debug a program. You probably know something about the BASIC programming language and probably have written at least one simple BASIC program (or could if you absolutely had to). If this is not true, I recommend that you spend some time with a more introductory text. All of IBM's books on BASIC cover this material very well.

Finally, because you're reading this, I also assume you have a curiosity about computer languages. You have probably discovered that computer languages are the lanterns in the caves of computing. You want to try out some of the lights that others have built and you want to learn how to build your own.

tiny-c, a very, very small language, doesn't have all the bells and whistles of a big commercial BASIC, nor does it have the concise expressive power of C. Because it is small, however, it is easy to understand thoroughly. When you are finished learning about tiny-c, not only will you have another lantern to guide you, but you will know enough about lantern construction to start designing your own.

This book has two goals. The first is to introduce you to structured programming and the C programming language. The second is to acquaint you, by means of two well-documented examples, with computer programs which implement computer languages. Let me spend a little time elaborating on these goals so you know exactly where we're headed (and where we're not).

FROM BASIC TO tiny-c TO C

The tiny-c language is a very, very restricted subset of the C programming language, but it captures just those essential elements of C which make C different from BASIC. While you can write usable programs in tiny-c, if you find these elements productive we encourage you to find out more about C itself. You will find not only that C has many features which tiny-c does not have, but also that C programs run much, much faster than tiny-c programs.

In a strict sense (the sense of a piece of mathematical reasoning called Turing's Theorem) you can't do anything with tiny-c—or even C, for that matter—that you can't do with BASIC. But we humans tend to do things that are easy, while avoiding things that are hard. Therefore, when you are picking a language for a program, it is wise to ask yourself, "What am I going to be doing most often in writing this program?" Will you be evaluating equations? Generating complicated printed output? Performing detailed manipulation of elaborate internal data structures? Are you going to be keeping track of lots of facts and trying to reason about them? After you have determined what you are mostly going to be doing, pick a language that makes the doing easy. Even if you don't already know the language, you will find that the time it takes you to learn the new language and then write your program will be less than the time it takes you to write the program in a familiar language that runs against the natural grain of your problem.

What tiny-c and C are particularly well-suited for is writing programs that live very close to the computers themselves. Operating systems, text editors, database managers, compilers, interpreters, and spreadsheets are all examples of programs that succeed when they can squeeze the maximum out of their host computer. One way to think of tiny-c and C is that they are understandable, portable, maintainable alternatives to assembly language.

COMPUTER LANGUAGE PROCESSING

The two programs we will study in this book—the tiny-c Shell and the tiny-c Interpreter—are examples of programs that implement or realize a computer language. This means that when they are given a statement in the language, the programs do what the language says the statement means.

The language handled by the tiny-c Shell is called a *command language* because the statements of the language are of the general forms "Do this," "Do that," and "Do this again." Each statement is processed by the program as soon as it is received; a new command can't be accepted until the processing of the last command is done. The activity that is caused by the command may still be going on when the new statement is given, but the processing of the old command has been completed.

The commands you give to your IBM DOS at the

```
A>
```

prompt are statements in a command language. You are commanding DOS to do something. If you say

```
A>copy c: / text / tiny-c / chapter1 / section1.rno a: / chapter1
```

you expect the DOS program to copy the first file into the second directory because that's what the statement means. If you say

```
A>print section1.doc
```

then you expect the file **section1.doc** to be shipped to the printer for printing. When you get the **A>** prompt back the file may still be printing, but the processing of the command itself is complete.

The language handled by the tiny-c Interpreter is called a *programming language*. The primary difference between a command language and a programming language is what happens when you hit the carriage return key. As we have seen, in a command language the computer immediately starts doing what you told it to do. This isn't true for a programming language. When you issue a statement in a programming language, the computer sort of makes a note of it. "Uh, huh," "Oh, yes I see," "Very good," and "Indeed." You have to say explicitly, "Do it!" to activate a program that understands the language and can execute all the statements you've entered.

And to whom do you say this? To a command language program, of course. That's just his cup of tea. One of the things a command language program should be able to do is to run a program which understands collections of programming language statements. This is just exactly what happens when you type

```
A>BASIC myfile
```

to DOS. You are saying, "Mr. DOS, I have brought together a file full of statements in the BASIC programming language called **myfile**. Would you please call up a program called 'BASIC' which understands these statements, and give the file to him so he will execute the statements and cause what they say to happen? And thank you very much." DOS accepts statements in a command language and BASIC accepts statements in a programming language. One of the command language statements you can give DOS is to tell BASIC about a file full of programming language statements that need processing.

In tiny-c, the tiny-c Shell corresponds to DOS and the tiny-c Interpreter corresponds to BASIC. But here's the neat part: The tiny-c command language program (the tiny-c Shell) is itself written in tiny-c programming language, and hence is being run by the tiny-c Interpreter. It's as if DOS were written in BASIC. This means that the program you command to find a program to interpret your tiny-c programming language statements is, at that very moment, being run by the very program you are asking it to find. (Did you stay with me?) "Hey, give that program that's running you this other stuff to run too, OK?" Most Lisp programming systems use this technique and it has proved very, very useful.

The magic rabbit hole is called **MC 11**. It's where a program can pass life (i.e., execution by the interpreter) along. Keep your eyes and your mind peeled for it.

ORGANIZATION OF THIS BOOK

The first order of business is acquainting you with tiny-c, kind of getting the general lay of the land. This is done in Chapter 1. We will study three tiny-c programs and show you how to use the tiny-c programming system. At the end of the chapter you should actually be able to write a tiny-c program on your own. In Chapter 1 we also spend a good deal of time talking about tiny-c programming style. This is important, since it gives you a feel for the kinds of programs that are well-suited for rendering in tiny-c and C, as well as a feel for the programs that are not.

In Chapter 2 we describe the tiny-c programming language in grisly detail. While you could probably write a tiny-c program when you finish Chapter 1, you will certainly have a lot of questions about exactly what the language does in various situations. Most of these questions should be answered by the time you finish Chapter 2.

After learning about tiny-c, in Chapter 3 we will study a nontrivial command language processing program written in tiny-c. It's the very program you will have been using to enter, edit, save, restore, and run tiny-c programs. This program is the tiny-c Shell. From the moment you start to use it you will be generating ideas on how it can

SLOAN

be improved. Since it is written in tiny-c and you will have learned how to program in tiny-c, you can get right to work changing your Shell to make it suit your tastes.

Finally, in Chapter 4 we examine a programming language processing program. It's the tiny-c Interpreter. This is the program which actually executes programs written in the tiny-c language. It is written in the C programming language. As I'm sure you will think of ways to improve the tiny-c language, you will have some incentive to learn C. Then you can modify the tiny-c Interpreter and bring your ideas alive.

As you can see, this book is a trip of four legs:

Leg 1: Using the tiny-c Shell.
Leg 2: Using the tiny-c language.
Leg 3: Understanding the tiny-c Shell program.
Leg 4: Understanding the tiny-c language Interpreter.

When you are all done, you will know tiny-c through and through. You can either adapt it to your own needs or go on to bigger and better things—like C. Whichever way you go, you will have climbed inside the world of computer language processing and begun to find your way around.

A final note: As we run into technical terms we will, of course, try to define them. Sometimes, however, we will not have toured all the conceptual outcroppings we must visit to formulate a full and complete definition. In such cases, we will make up a definition that keeps us going, but may be only part of the whole story. Sometimes it might even be a simplification bordering on a white lie. To quote Don Knuth, "Once you understand a simple but false rule, it will not be hard to supplement that rule with its exceptions."

tiny c 1

tiny-c Programming

In this chapter you will learn how to use the tiny-c Shell to create, edit, save, restore, run, and debug tiny-c programs. In the process, of course, you will start to learn something about the tiny-c programming language.

I urge you to load tiny-c into your PC or PCjr and use tiny-c as you read about it. You can't hurt anything and you'll be generating lots of questions and problems which will help you get more out of what you are reading.

HELLO, WORLD

Here's a tiny tiny-c program:

```
hello_world [
pl "Hello, world"
]
```

Why don't you load the tiny-c disk into your computer and start the **tinyc** program? When the tiny-c prompt appears

```
tc>
```

type this little three-line program in? Like this:

```
tc>hello_world [
tc>   pl "Hello, world"
tc>]
```

Be careful! The character between the **o** and the **w** is an underscore (__), not a minus (–). The underscore is a shifted minus.

What is there to notice about this program? First, it has a name. Its name is **hello__world**. To run the program named **hello__world**, all you have to do is type its name right after a period. The period says, "Do this!"

```
tc>.hello_world
Hello, world
tc>
```

Is this what happened to you? If it did, you're cooking with gas; if not, then you didn't enter the program properly. What you should do in this case is jump ahead to the next section and find out how to edit what you have typed in. Edit **hello_world** until it behaves like this and then rejoin us here. You'll be able to breeze through the next section when we come to it, so you won't lose any time.

PROGRAMS, FUNCTIONS, AND STATEMENTS

What is it that **hello_world** names? Well, we see a pair of matched brackets,**[** and **]**, surrounding an instruction that seems to cause the words "Hello, world" to be printed out on the screen. The character string **hello_world** names everything between these two brackets.

In order to accomplish anything of any reasonable complexity, we will need lots of named program pieces such as **hello_world**, each doing some small, well-defined part of the overall task. Let's agree to use the word *program* to refer to the entire collection of pieces that gets the whole job done. Let's use the word *function* to refer to any one piece. Finally, let's call *statements* the individual instructions that make up these pieces and actually do something.

So **hello_world** is a tiny-c function that contains one statement which prints out "Hello, world."

FUNCTIONS CALL FUNCTIONS CALL FUNCTIONS CALL . . .

Notice how **hello_world** does its thing. It uses another tiny-c function named **pl**. When one function uses another, the using function is said to *call* the used function. "Hey, **pl**. Do this for me." The **pl** tiny-c function is built into the tiny-c system library. (There are lots of useful functions like **pl** in the system library. We'll describe them all in Chapter 2.) As you probably have guessed, **pl** simply prints what it is given on a new line. The string **pl** stands for **print_on_a_new_line**. The thing that you give a function—"Hello, world" in the case at hand—is called the *argument* of the function. Function **pl** looks for only one argument and it prints out whatever it gets; other functions look for two or three or more.

This is the heart-of-hearts of tiny-c and C: functions which call other functions which call other functions to get the job done. Each function is kind of a stitching-together of specific requests to other functions to do particular tasks. Functions get other functions to do particular tasks by passing them arguments. "Hello, world" was the argument that **hello_world** passed to **pl**. The **pl** function knows how to print out any line it is given. Function **hello_world** used it to print out a particular line; namely, "Hello, world."

Actually, this passing of the buck isn't so strange. Think of what happens when you order a meal in a restaurant. You tell the waiter what you want to eat, he tells the cook what to cook, the cook tells the owner what to buy, the owner tells the food distributor what to deliver, the food distributor tells the packer what to ship, and the packer tells the farmer what to grow, the farmer tells the field hand what to plant . . .

and so it goes. Everybody calls everybody else, adds his or her own little bit, and passes the result along. Presto! Lo and behold, there's the fried pickle on your plate.

The beauty is that everyone does one generally useful thing well, rather than trying to do everything just adequately. This makes for a much more efficient, productive and tractable system for both people and computer programs.

That's what *structured programming* is all about—building large, efficient, tractable programs. And that's why you're learning tiny-c.

EDITING A tiny-c PROGRAM

The program you are talking to when you start tiny-c is called *the tiny-c Shell.* It is a command language processing program that lets you create, edit, run, debug, save, and restore programs written in the tiny-c programming language. In this section you will learn how to use the tiny-c Shell. There are only twelve commands that the Shell understands, so this really isn't much of an undertaking.

Fundamentals of the Shell

The tiny-c Shell announces its presence by printing the tiny-c prompt:

```
tc>
```

indicating it is ready for you to command it what to do. You can now type lines of your tiny-c program or give commands for the Shell to execute.

Any line you type must end with a carriage return; the Shell does nothing with your input line until the carriage return is given.

After you enter a carriage return, the Shell will either enter the line into your program or execute the command. Then it gives you another prompt

```
tc>
```

and awaits another line or command.

If you mistype before giving a carriage return, the backspace key (the key marked with a single arrow pointing to the left, right above the carriage return key) kills the most recently typed character; you can press it several times to kill several characters.

If you mistype a line so hopelessly that you want to do the whole line over, then the escape (Esc) key kills the whole line. It must be given before you press carriage return, however. You cannot press it several times to kill several lines. It will delete only the line for which you have not yet given a carriage return.

If you have typed a carriage return and still want to make a change, this can be done. You must explicitly delete the line, using the delete command described below. Then you can re-enter the line.

Do not type in line numbers at the beginning of each line. The tiny-c Shell does not use them; in fact, it does not even tolerate them.

To indent, use tabs or spaces. The use of indentation to show the number of logical conditions in effect at each point in a program can greatly improve its readability.

Now you've probably asked yourself, "How does the Shell tell the difference between a command and a line of text?" Good question!

- *A command always begins with a period, a plus, or a minus. Anything else is a text line.*

We will cover Shell commands later; first, we will go over text lines. To do this we need the concepts of *program buffer, line zero,* and *current line.*

As you enter program lines, they are collected into an area of the computer's memory called the *program buffer.* Think of the program buffer as a series of text lines. As you enter new text lines, they do into the program buffer. Each new line can be appended to the end of all the lines that are already in the buffer. Or it may go at the beginning of all the lines that are already there. Or it may go between lines that are already in the buffer.

When you start out, the program buffer contains only one line. It is called *line zero.* Line zero has no text; it's just a carriage return. No matter what else you put into the program buffer, line zero is always there and is always just a carriage return.

There is one particular line in the program buffer which you should think of as the *current line.* It is where you are located . . . where your attention is focused . . . no, actually where the Shell's attention is focused . . . in the program buffer.

Initially the current line is line zero. You can always display the current line by giving the print command:

```
tc>.p
```

The tc > is the prompt printed by the Shell. The .p is the print command you typed in. The current line is printed on the screen immediately after you type .p and give a carriage return.

Entering Text Lines

Now, where do new text lines go? Here's the rule used by the Shell:

- *A text line is entered into the program buffer immediately after the current line. The newly entered line becomes the current line.*

As you recall, line zero is the current line when you start off. Let's say you type a text line. According to this rule, it will go into the program buffer after line 0, as line 1. It also becomes the current line. You type a second text line. It goes in after the current line (line 1) and becomes line 2. Now line 2 is current. If all you do is keep on entering text lines, they will each go into the program buffer one after the other. This is what you'd expect, no?

There are commands described below which makes any line in the program buffer the current line. As we have seen, whenever you enter a series of text lines, each is inserted one after the other below the current line. Thus by moving around you can enter text lines anywhere in the program buffer. You will discover that this text line entry rule is simple, natural, and powerful.

The Shell Commands

In the description of the Shell commands below, an n represents an integer with no leading plus or minus sign; for example, 5 but neither +5 nor −5. Exactly one blank must separate an integer **n** from preceding characters.

tc>.p	Print the current line on the screen.
tc>.p n	Print **n** lines starting with the current line. The last line printed becomes the current line.
tc>.d	Delete the current line. Make the line *before* it the current line.
tc>.d n	Delete **n** lines starting with the current line. Make the line *before* the first deleted line the current line.
tc> +	Move down one line and make the line *after* the present current line the new current line.
tc> +n	Move down **n** lines; the new current line is the present current line plus **n**.
tc> −	Move up one line; make the line *before* the present current line the new current line.
tc> −n	Move up **n** lines; the new current line is the present current line minus **n**.
tc>.n	Make the **n**th line in the program buffer the current line; in other words go to line **n**
tc>.l text	Starting with the line *after* the current line (proceeding to the end of the program buffer if necessary), locate a line containing **text**. If found, print the line and make it current; if not found, print "?" and leave the current line unchanged. There must be one blank between the "l" and the first character of **text**. A circumflex (∧) as the first character of **text** means the text must begin the line. A ∧ as the last character of **text** means the text must end the line. The text may contain blanks.
tc>.l	Same as above, but use the same **text** as given in the previous locate or change command.
tc>.c text newtext	In the current line the first occurrence of **text** is replaced by **newtext**. If **text** does not occur in the current line, then no change is made. In either case the resulting line is printed and the current line remains the current line.

As shown, there are exactly two blanks in the command, one after the **c**, and one between **text** and **new text**. In this form, no blanks can be used in **text** or **newtext** because a blank is the delimiter that separates them. However, since you may want to manipulate text containing blanks, any character can be used as the delimiter.

For example, the command can be given as:

```
tc >.c/text/newtext
```

In this case, blanks can be used in the texts, but virgules (slashes) may not be used. An optional delimiter is permitted at the end of **newtext**:

```
tc >.c/text/newtext/
```

Either **text** or **newtext** can be empty.

```
tc >.c//newtext/
```

will insert **newtext** at the beginning of the line. The form

```
tc >.c/text//
```

will erase **text** from the current line.

Finally, when making a series of identical changes, you need not retype the text over and over. The form

```
tc>.c
```

Makes a change on the current line, substituting the **newtext** given in the most recent change command for the **text** given in the most recent change or locate command. The carriage return must be immediately after the **c**.

This is all you can do with the change command. What are some other commands you can give the Shell?

tc>./ — Prints the current line number, the total number of lines, the total number of characters used in the program buffer, and the total number of unused characters. This reminds you where you are in the program buffer and tells you something about how full the buffer is.

tc>.r file_name — Reads the file named **file_name** from the disk, putting what is read *after* the last line. The current line is not changed. **Read** is like the LOAD command in BASIC5.

tc>.w file_name — Writes all lines in the program buffer to the disk, giving the name **file_name** to what is written. **Write** is like the SAVE command in BASIC.

RUNNING A tiny-c PROGRAM

How do you run a tiny-c program? Remember the "Do it!" dot that we used to run **hello_world**?

- *A command starting with a period followed by at least two alphabetic characters is executed immediately as a tiny-c statement.*

We will learn about tiny-c statements in the next chapter, but you have probably guessed already that a function call is a perfectly legal tiny-c statement. Therefore, to execute a tiny-c function you just mention its name after a period.

Now you know the whole truth about running **hello_world**. When you entered

```
tc>.hello_world
```

what you really did, perhaps without even knowing it, is call the **hello_world** function.

Can arguments be passed to functions you call with a period, she asked in whispered tones. Is a worm icky? Try this:

```
tc>.pl "hello, world"
```

What happened, and went on to cause that to happen? You called the **pl** system library function and passed to it the argument"hello, world", that's what went on.

The "Do it!" dot rule turns the tiny-c Shell into a handy-dandy personal calculator. To add 7 and 11 and print the answer, call the **pn (print_number)** system library function with the argument 7 + 11, like this:

```
tc>.pn 7+11
```

Try it and see what happens. And now try some other arithmetic expressions.

The ramifications of the "Do it!" dot rule are really quite surprising. As you build up generally useful functions in the program buffer, reflect on how they might be used in this immediate execution mode. In addition to simply calling a function, you will discover that you can also write one-line tiny-c programs that are immediately executed by the "Do it!" dot rule. Here's an example to whet your appetite:

```
tc  .[char c;c='a' -1;while ((c=c+1)   ='z') putchar c]
```

Don't worry if you don't understand it. Just tuck it away as a little treat to come back to when you've learned a little more.

Bumping the Top and the Bottom

Several commands can bump into the top or the bottom of the program buffer.This is all right; in fact, it can be quite useful. For example, suppose there are 50 or so lines in the buffer. Then

```
tc>.0
tc>.p 999
```

makes line zero current and then prints the whole buffer. When the print command bumps into the bottom of the buffer it stops. The commands **.d**, **+**, **−**, **.n**, and **.l** can also bump into the top or the bottom. A convenient way to go to the last line in the program buffer is:

```
tc>.999
```

Issuing the command

```
tc>./
```

at this juncture will tell you how big your program is.

Deleting

Line zero cannot be deleted. To delete lines at the top, go to line 1, and give a deletion command that gets rid of the number of lines you want to discard. Remember that deletion moves the current line up, not down. In this way, new lines you type right after giving a delete will replace the lines you deleted. Neat footwork, eh?

Line Numbers

When lines are inserted or deleted, lines further down in the buffer immediately get different line numbers. So .n is not the best way to hop to your favorite line landmark. The best way is to use the .l command to locate it.

Recall the hello_world function:

```
hello_world [
pl "Hello, world"
]
```

The command:

```
tc>.2
```

makes the second line—the line with pl on it—the current line. But if edits are made to hello_world, then this line may or may not continue to be the second line. For this reason, locate is a more powerful program buffer navigation tool.

Using Locate and Change

Locating all lines with a given text is done like this:

```
tc>.0
tc>.l world
```

The first command hops to line 0. This is always safe, since line zero never changes. (It's always that carriage return at the beginning of the program, remember?) The next command will match line 1 in the hello_world function, since "world" is part of the name of the function hello_world. If you then say

```
tc>.l
```

you will match line 2, since "world" appears in "Hello, world."

In a longer program, continuing to enter.l will locate each subsequent instance of the text you are seeking. In this particular case, of course, you're out of "worlds" and any more .l's earn you a "?" when you bump the bottom.

Making a common change throughout the buffer is just as easy. To change"world" to "galaxy," you would enter

```
tc>.0
tc>.l world
```

This will make line 1 current. Now you type

```
tc >.c world galaxy
```

The "hello_world in line 1 is now changed to "hello_galaxy." Continue with tc >.l to find the next instance of "world." This will make line 2 current since it contains "world." Change "world" to "galaxy" by typing:

```
tc >.c
```

and resume with:

```
tc>.l
```

to find the next occurrence of "world."

You can continue in this fashion, changing lines selectively, until you again bump the bottom. When you do, you will have changed all appearances of "world" to "galaxy."

Errors

Sometimes . . . just sometimes . . . when you run a tiny-c program an error will be detected. When this happens,the program halts and the Shell resumes control of the situation. Your program text is intact; you can edit it or restart it or write it to a disk.

The Shell prints three lines of helpful information about what happened and then gives you its prompt:

```
17 — err 26
text of bad line
        <
tc >
```

The first line shows the line number on which the error occurred and the error number. Consult Appendix B for the explanation that goes with each error number. The second line is the text of the bad line. Immediately above or to the left of the < on the third line is where the problem was discovered. This may or may not be the real problem, depending on the logic of the program.

THE NUMBER GUESSING GAME

Type the following:

```
tc>.1
tc>.d 999
```

This clears out the program buffer. Convince yourself of this by typing

```
tc>./
```

The response should be

```
0 0 0 12000
```

which means that there are 0 lines in the program buffer, the current line is 0, you have used 0 characters, and there are 12,000 characters left.That's a clean slate, my friend.

Now type in Listing 1-1 just as it appears. I know it sounds as exciting as Bingo night in Cleveland, but please do it. In the next section we're going discuss the program you're entering in detail and you really do need to get some experience with the Shell.

Warning: Twenty-two lines into this exercise you will see

```
tc >.r random
```

What you are doing here is causing the file RANDOM to be read in from the disk and appended to the end of what you have typed in so far. Be sure that your tiny-c disk is still inserted or tiny-c won't be able to find the file.

You've already seen a very short tiny-c function—**hello_world**—and you just learned how to use the tiny-c Shell to compose and edit tiny-c programs. Let's take a close look at that program you just finished typing (broken out of the entry dialogue as Listing 1-2) and start learning about the tiny-c language.

How does this program work? Let's go through the program line-by-line.This is called a *program walk-through*.

A Walk Through the Guessnum Function

Starting at the top, the first line is a *comment*. A comment starts with /* and goes to the end of the line. A comment line is there for humans only. It is ignored by the computer when you run your program. A comment is there to remind *you* what your program does when you run it.

The next line contains the name of a function, together with the opening bracket of the pair of brackets that enclose the statements that make up the function. The function which follows is called **guessnum**.

Following **guessnum** is a compound statement which is 12 lines long. The compound statement ends with the line that reads:

```
]      /* end of program
```

In other words, the compound statement is everything between balanced left-right brackets. This compound statement is called the *body* of the function **guessnum**.

The first *simple statement* in **guessnum** is:

```
int guess, number
```

This statement brings into being two *integer variables* names **guess** and number. All variables in tiny-c must be announced or declared before they can be used. When executed, the **int** statement will create the two variables and give them an initial value of zero.

The second simple statement in **guessnum** is

```
number = random (1,100)
```

This statement sets the value of the variable **number** equal to the value of the tiny-c function **random** when it is executed with its first argument equal to 1 and its second argument equal to 100. The function **random**, which we will discuss later in detail, returns a random number that lies between its two arguments. In this case, it will return a random number between 1 and 100.

Listing 1-1. Entry dialogue for the Number Guessing Game program.

```
tc >/* Guess a number between 1 andg100
tc >.c/q//
/* Guess a number between 1 and 100
tc >guessnum[
tc > int guess, number
tc > number=random(1,100)
tc >  pl "guess a number between 1 and 100"
tc > pl "tyype in your guess now"
tc >  while(guess != number) [
tc >  guess = gn
tc >  if (guess == number) pl "right!"
tc >  if (guess tc > number)plq"too high"
tc >  if (guess < number) pl "too low"
tc >  pl ""; pl " "
tc >  ] /* end of game loop
tc >  ] /* end of program
tc >./

14  14  380  11620

tc >.1
/*Guess a number between 1 and 100
tc >.p 99
/* Guess a number between 1 and 100
guessnum[
  int guess, number
  number=random(1,100)
  pl "guess a number between 1 and 100"
  pl "tyype in your guess now"
  while(guess != number) [
    guess = gn
    if (guess == number) pl "right!"
    if (guess tc > number) plq "too high"
    if (guess < number) pl "too low"
    pl " ";pl" "
  ] /* end of game loop
] /* end of program

tc >.r random
  292
  14 25 672 11328
tc >.p
]    /* end of program
tc >+
```

```
/* random — generates a random number between little and big
tc   .p 99
/* random — generates a random number between little and big
int seed,last
random int little.big [
  int range
if (last= =0) last=seed=99
range=big-little+'1
last=last*seed
if (last<0) last = -last
return little + (last/8)%range
]
tc   .guessnum

guess a number between 1 and 100
tyype in your guess now50

10 - - - err 26
if (guess tc > number) plq"too high"

tc >.c/q/ /
     if (guess tc > number) pl "too high"
tc >.0

tc> .1 yy
  pl "tyype in your guess now"
tc> .c/yy/y/
  pl "type in your guess now"
tc> .guessnum
guess a number between 1 and 100
type in your guess now50
too high
25
too low
37
too high
27
too high
26
right!
tc >.w guess
  2 25 671 11329
  671
tc>
```

Listing 1-2. The Number Guessing Game.

```
/* Guess a number between 1 and 100
guessnum [
  int guess, number
  number = random (1,100)
  pl "guess a number between 1 and 100"
  pl "type in your guess now"
  while (guess != number) [
    guess = gn
    if (guess == number) pl "right!"
    if (guess > number) pl "too high"
    if (guess < number) pl "too low"
pl " "; pl " "
]    /* end of game loop
]    /* end of program

/* random-generates a random number between little and big
int seed, last
random int little, big [
  int range
  if (seed == 0) seed = last = 99
  range = big - little + 1
  last = last * seed
  if (last < 0) last = - last
  return little + (last/8) % range
```

On the next two lines are calls to **pl**. We've already seen **pl** in the **hello_world** program. It is the system library function that prints a line; in fact it prints the quoted *string* that is its argument. The first call to **pl** will cause "guess a number between 1 and 100" to be printed out on your screen; the second call will cause "type in your guess now" to be printed.

The **while** statement on the seventh line sets up a *loop*. The general form of a **while** statement is:

> while (expression) statement

In this instance, the *expression* part of the **while** statement is

> guess != number

The pair of characters != mean "not equal to." Combined with the **while**, the first part of the statement could be read as

> while **guess** is not equal to **number**

The expression **guess != number** is evaluated; if it is true, the statement part of the **while** statement is performed and then the expression is evaluated again. If the expression **guess** != number is false, the statement is skipped.

You will recall that **guess** was set to 0 by the **int** statement. Further, **number** cannot be less than 1 because of what **random** does. Therefore the expression **guess != number** must be true the first time it is encountered. The result is that the statement part of the **while** is executed.

This statement is, in fact, another compound statement. It is composed of six simple statements. The first of these statements is

```
guess = gn
```

The function **gn** is system library function like **pl**. The name stands for "get_a_number." When **gn** is called, it reads a number typed at the keyboard and returns that value. So here the program waits until you type a number and a carriage return. When this happens, the variable **guess** is assigned the number you typed.

The next three simple statements are **if** statements. The general form of the **if** statement is

if ***(expression) statement***

where the statement part is executed only if the expression part is true.

Can you figure out what these three **if** statements do? Try to read the statements aloud.

> if **guess** is equal to **number** then print "right"
> if **guess** is greater than **number** then print "too high"
> if **guess** is less than **number** then print "too low"

Do you begin to see how the program works?

Statements five and six of the **while** compound statement are of the form

```
pl""
```

Including a null string ("") makes **pl** go to a new line and print nothing. Notice that the semicolon allows you to write more than one simple statement on the same program line, so

```
pl"" ; pl""
```

prints two blank lines.

Now we are finally at the end of the **while** loop. Since the expression part of the **while** was true, the **while** statement is executed again. This starts with another evaluation of the expression

```
guess != number
```

to see if it is true or false. If the first guess is not equal to **number**, then the **while**'s compound statement is executed again. Another **guess** is read, the appropriate remark is made, and two more blank lines are printed; the **while** is done yet again.

Eventually you will get the right number and **guess** will be equal to **number**. This will cause a "right!" and two blank lines to be printed. The **while** condition is then tested again. The expression **guess != number** will be false, so the entire compound statement part of the while is skipped. This brings us to the end of **guessnum**. The game is over and the program stops.

Before we walk through **random**, notice that the variables **seed** and **last** are declared outside of both of the functions **guessnum** and **random**. They are called *global variables*. They will be created when the program is started. They are initially set to zero like variables that are declared inside functions. Because they aren't inside either **guessnum** or **random** they are accessible to both of them.

On the other hand, the variables **guess**, **number** and **range** are declared inside functions. They are called *local variables*. The variables **guess** and **number** are known and usable only within **guessnum** and **range** is local to **random**.

A Walk Through Random

The first line of **random** gives the function name as usual. But before the **[** marking the beginning of the body of **random**, the two integer arguments, **little** and **big**, are declared. A value must be supplied for each of these arguments when **random** is called. The call in the sixth line of **guessnum** sets **little** to 1 and **big** to 100.

Now we enter the body of the function **random**.The **range** variable is declared an integer and is initially zero. On the first call, **seed** is also zero. Now **seed** and **last** are both set to 99. The **range** is calculated and is 100. Variable **last** is set to the product of **last** and **seed**, which is 9801.This is not less than 0, so the statement part of the **if** is skipped.

We next come to the **return** statement. It does two things. First, it evaluates the expression

```
little + (last/8) % range.
```

The result is made the *value of the function*. Secondly, the **return** statement returns control to the program that called the function it appears in. In this case, it returns control to **guessnum** from **random**.

Expressions in tiny-c are similar to algebraic expressions. The plus symbol (+) means add, a slash (/) means divide, and minus (−) means subtract or take the negative. An asterisk (*) signifies multiplication. The percent sign (%) is an unusual symbol that means divide the left side by the right side and use the *remainder*, not the quotient. This is the same as the MOD operator in Pascal. For example,

```
1225 % 100
```

is 25.

Thus, the **return** statement calculates the expression:

```
little + (last/8) % range
    = 1 + (9801/8) remainder 100
    = 1 + 1225 remainder 100
    = 1 + 25
    = 26
```

The value 26 is returned as the value of function **random**. It also leaves 9801 in **last** and 99 in **seed**. Since these are global variables, their values are retained between function calls. This is not true of local variables like **range**. Their values are retained only during the execution of the function in which they are defined; when that function is exited, their values disappear.

Let's go around **random** once more. On a second call, **range** is recreated and reinitialized to zero. The variable **seed** is not zero this time, so **seed** and **last** are not set to 99, but remain 99 and 9801 respectively. The **range** is recalculated as 100. Then

```
last = last * seed
     = 9801 * 99
     = 980229
```

This number is too big for tiny-c.

Every computer has a limit on the size of the numbers that can be represented. Numbers in tiny-c must be in the range

```
-32768 <= tiny-c integer number <= 32767
```

The value of **last** *overflows* this range. It will be assigned the value –12741! (We explain this more completely in the next chapter.) A value of –12741 is less than 0, so the next statement assigns **last** the value 12741. Then the **return** statement calculates:

```
1 + (12741/8) remainder 100
  = 1 + 1592 remainder 100
  = 93
```

This time 93 is returned as the value of **random**.

Before pushing on, take a moment and go back over **guessnum**. Make sure you have some notion of what each statement does and what the overall layout of the program means. If something isn't clear and if the walk-through leaves you puzzled, jot down what bothers you. In the next chapter we define the tiny-c language in detail. Having questions like this at hand will help you connect what you are reading to what you are trying to understand.

tiny-c PROGRAMMING STYLE

Perhaps you have heard structured programming described as "GOTO-less" programming. Or programming with just "if-then-else" and "do-while" control statements. Although such remarks oversimplify what structured programming is all about, they don't miss the mark altogether.

The essence of structured programming is *program clarity*. You can write programs in small, modular parts and easy-to-follow program flow. You can use well-chosen, descriptive variable names. This leads to clear, understandable programs. Program clarity is really what structured programming is all about.

We discuss here four principal ideas of structured programming found in tiny-c that make program clarity possible.These are:

- Modularity
- Predictable program flow
- Local variables
- Meaningful variable names

Modularity in software is just as important as modularity in hardware. Sticking to this principle makes it possible to deal with complexity. A module is a brick or atom used for building bigger modules. Seen from within, a module may be very complex, but from the outside it is an indivisible whole. Software modularity in tiny-c is achieved through the use of *functions*.

Program flow is predictable if you can point to any statement and easily answer the question, "Under what conditions is this statement executed?" This is particularly important if the program is 20 or 30 pages long and still has bugs. Poring over the whole program and drawing arrows is not an easy way to answer the question. Predictable program flow can be achieved in many ways. In tiny-c, it is done with *compound statements* and the absence of a GOTO statement.

Functions also make it possible to hide variables used in a strictly local context. The variable n is very popular; it is used frequently to count things. Have you ever had a BASIC program blow up because you were using n in two places for two different purposes? The fix was to change one of them to n1.

A better idea is *local* and *global* variables. Local variables are known only within the function that defines them; global variables are known everywhere. In BASIC, all variables are global variables. That's why you can only have one n. In tiny-c, two functions can declare their own local variables named n and they won't get confused. There will be two n's; one used exclusively inside one function and one used exclusively inside the other.

As for *long, meaningful names* for variables and functions, just look at the sample programs to see the improvement. The tiny-c statement

```
if(klingons_in_sector > torpedos_remaining) fire_phasers
```

certainly tells you more about what is going on than

```
535 IF KL > TL THEN GOSUB 5400
```

David Gries suggests structured programming be called "simplicity theory," and characterizes it as "an approach to understanding the complete programming process." As a pleasant dividend, structured programming is more enjoyable than monolithic programming. It should, therefore, certainly be a part of personal computing. To begin our look at tiny-c as a structured programming language, let's look at the foundation of functions and predictable program flow—the compound statement.

Compound Statements

When you write a program, you write a sequence of statements:

```
x = x-1
a = b+c
b = b*2-c
x = b-a
```

The idea behind a compound statement is to make one statement out of a collection of statements, just as atoms go together to make a molecule. This is done in tiny-c by simply putting square brackets around the atoms:

```
[x  = x-1
a   = b+c
b   = b*2-c
x   = b-a]
```

Anywhere you can write a simple statement, you can also write a compound statement. This sounds simple but the effect is far-reaching. For example, most programming languages have an if statement similar to this:

if (*expression*) *statement*

So you can write

```
if (x>0) x = x-1
```

But compound the statement part and you have this capability:

```
if (x >0) [
b = b*2-c
a = b+c
x = x-1
]
```

This multi-line if is not some special kind of if. It is still our old friend

if (*expression*) *statement*

but the statement part is compound. The compound statement is treated as an indivisible unit. It is either all done or not done at all depending on the value of the expression.

The compound statement also is a natural for *loops*. There is a big difference among the various programming languages in how you write loops, but they all have one thing in common. A loop has a beginning and an end. A compound statement can be used to express this fact.

The tiny-c looping statement is

while (*expression*) *statement*

Notice the similarity with the if; only the keyword has changed. Here's how while works. The expression is evaluated. If it is true, the statement is executed, and then the while is done again. The effect is a repeated if, i.e., a loop. As long as the expression remains true, the statement is done again and again. This loop will continue forever or until something in the statement causes the expression to become false.

As usual, the statement can be compound, as in

```
while (x>0) [
a = b+c
b = b*2-c
x = x-1
]
```

The compound statement is a natural way to delimit the beginning and end of loops.

With one simple idea, the compound statement, we achieve quite a bit. The if statement is more powerful than is common in non-structured programming languages, and the concept of a loop collapses to a simple repeated if or while statement. In both situations you are stating exactly the conditions under which the statement—whether simple or compound—is to be executed.

This is how compound statements create predictable program flow. You can always see the conditions that must prevail for a statement to be executed.

Nesting Compound Statements

Here's the rule that gives compound statements their power:

- *Anywhere you can write a simple statement, you can write a compound statement.*

That is a fundamental rule. A compound statement contains simple statements. Therefore a compound statement can contain compound statements. The following code fragment illustrates this point.

```
[ x = x-1
  a = b+c
  b = b*2-a
  x = b-a
]
```

The statement a=b+c is a simple statement. The rule says a compound statement can be written here. For example:

```
[ x = x-1
  [  a = b+c
     w = y+2*x+w
     y = 17
  ]
  b = b*2-a
  x = b-a
]
```

The above substitution of a compound for a simple statement is certainly allowable but is of no practical value.

The real utility in nested compounds is in writing nested **if** and **while** statements. The following code is a more realistic example of the use of nested compound statements.

```
if (x>0) [
  while (x   limit) [
      if (case= =1) [
         y = 0; w = 99
      ]
      if (case= =2) [
         y = 99; w = 0
      ]
      next action
      x = x+1
  ]
]
```

If you remove everything except the brackets from this code, you have:

```
[ [ [ ] [ ] ] ]
```

This is what is meant by *nested* compound statements. Brackets are used to form program units the same way parentheses are used to create arithmetic statements. The main difference is that a pair of brackets is preceded by a function name or an expression. In the first case, you're naming the contents of the brackets; in the second, you're stating the conditions under which the contents are to be executed.

Predictable Program Flow

Look at the y = 0 statement in the fourth line of the last example. How can it be reached? Only if case is 1 and x is less than limit. You simply can't get here otherwise.

How can nextaction be reached? Only if x is less than limit—and then only after possible changes to y and w. This program has simple, predictable flow. The only way a statement other than a while can be reached is from directly above. The while statements can also be reached from their matching] below.

Indenting and the Placement of Brackets

Brackets define the structure of a program. Indenting means nothing. But one of the purposes of structured programming is to make programs more readable and more understandable by you. A good choice of indenting style is very important to program readability. There are several styles from which to choose. The actual choice is not too important, but once you choose a style, stick to it. Consistency *is* important.

One easily explained style is to align matching brackets vertically, like this:

```
  if (x<0)
[  statement
   statement
   statement
   statement
   statement
]
```

A problem with this is that when editing the first statement, care must be taken to keep the [intact, so some use this style:

```
  if (x<0)
[
  statement
  statement
  statement
  statement
  statement
]
```

This takes an extra line. Also, there is a visual break between the if and its statement.

To remedy this situation, some programmers take the left bracket and move it to the end of the preceding line:

```
if (x<0) [
   statement
   statement
   statement
   statement
   statement
]
```

The right bracket is now vertically aligned with the **if** or **while** that preceded the compound statement.

You may pick one of these or invent a style of your own. But remember, whatever you decide to do, do it consistently.

FUNCTIONS

A large software project can usually be broken into natural parts, with each part being programmed and debugged as a separate unit. Each of these units then becomes a reliable building block for the construction of still larger parts of the project. Sometimes units can be designed to be useful in many projects.

In various programming languages these building blocks are called *subprograms* or *subroutines*. In tiny-c they're called *functions*. Here is a tiny-c function for any computer-versus-human game

```
game [
      getready
      while (stillplaying) [
          humanturn
          if (stillplaying) computerturn
        ]
        gameover
  ]
```

The name of the function is **game**. The compound statement that follows is called the *body* of the function. Each **[** can be read as "do all of this," and its matching **]** read as "end of this."

Function **game** divides the design of a game program into five parts:

getready	initializes things, and prints instructions if requested.
stillplaying	determines if the game is still going, and returns a value of true if it is.
humanturn	conducts the human's turn.
computerturn	conducts the computer's turn.
gameover	computes and prints scores, makes remarks about the human's skill, promotes the human, or whatever.

The **game** function is the first step in "divide-and-conquer" or "top-down" program development.

Let's carry this development one step further. The **getready** function can be expanded this way

```
        getready [
          ps "Do you want instructions?"
          if (gc = = 'y') instructions
          setupboard
    ]
```

Function **getready** divides the initialization into two parts, **instructions** and **setupboard.** (In case you're wondering, **ps** and **gc** are system library functions. The **ps** function prints a character string and **gc** reads a character.) The construction

= = 'y'

tests if the character is a "y."

Notice that **game** and **getready** are universal and can be used in many game programs. Programming in this fashion eventually leads to a library of useful, general-purpose functions. These can be pulled off the shelf and into a software project. You know they work because you used them before. Your programming becomes more productive and more pleasant.

The next time you're programming a sizable project—anything more than a page—try to identify subsets of the logic usable in other projects. Capture these as functions. It is gratifying to discover a general-purpose function where none was suspected.

LOCAL AND GLOBAL VARIABLES

A *local variable* is one that is known only inside a function. It can be used and changed only within the body of the function. Even its name is unknown outside the function. In fact, its name can be used in other functions without conflict. This is what makes local variables useful.

Take a look at the following code example. There are four local variables in these two functions. The variables **n** and **maximum** are local to **a_function.** The variables **n** and **total** are local to **another_function.** If either of these functions calls the other, the values of **n** will not be confused because they have meaning only inside the body of their respective functions. It helps to think of local variable names as being preceded by the possessive form of the function to which they are local. For example, **a_function's n** and **another_function's n.**

```
a_function [
      int n, maximum
      n=0
      while (n      maximum) [
            n = n+1
      ]
]
another_function [
      int n, total
      n = n+2
      total = total+n
]
```

The value of locals is obvious to anyone who has spent a nasty debugging session trying to find out where in a huge program some variable is getting changed.

Cases may arise in which two functions have to share some information, but neither is on the call path to the other. In this case one can use a *global* variable to contain the shared information. Global variables should be used sparingly because they can cause debugging headaches. Choosing good, descriptive names for globals helps to alleviate this problem. A global named **k** invites disaster. Call it **klingons_left** and you're less likely to use it accidentally for two different purposes. Also, you've given yourself a pretty good reminder of the variable's meaning.

MORSE CODE GENERATOR

There are only two ways to learn a new programming language:

1) Study programs written in the language.
2) Write programs in the language.

In the beginning, it is more important to study programs written by people who are fluent in the language than it is to generate a lot of new code. In this way you learn the feel of the natural grain of the language without getting entangled in all the rules of its formation. It is much easier to understand the rules after you have seen them in action. After all, can you imagine insisting that a child learn the rules of English grammar before you began to speak with her?

The tiny-c system library for the IBM PC and PCjr contains a function called **beep**. This function takes two arguments; the first argument says what the frequency of the beep should be in cycles per second. The second argument says how long the beep should be in tenths of seconds. For example,

```
beep(523, 10)
```

sounds a middle C for one second.

In this last section of our introduction to tiny-c we present a program that is useful, easy to read, and clearly exhibits the spirit of the tiny-c language. It is a Morse code program that uses the **beep** function to generate letters in Morse code. This program has an interesting property: it is really two programs in one.

One Morse code program allows you to practice receiving individual letters in Morse code. Type

```
tc>.practice
```

to practice. Answer the four questions. The answer to the last question initializes the random number generator so you get different letters each time you practice. Now write down the letters beeped to you in Morse code. At the end, compare your answers with the ones displayed.

To use the second Morse code program, have a friend type

```
tc>.morse "any message whatever"
```

and try to decode the message being sent to you.

Listing 1-3 contains the Morse code program. Before running the program read it over. Try to understand how it works. This shouldn't be difficult if there's any truth in everything we've been claiming for structured programming and tiny-c. Not only will you be able to use the program more effectively if you understand how it works, but, as you get ideas about how the program can be improved, you will be able to add your ideas to the program and make it do exactly what you want it to.

Listing 1-3. Morse Code Generator program.

```
int SPEED

dot [
  beep (440. 2)
  pause
]

dash [
  beep (440, 6)
  pause
]

pause[
  int k
  while ((k=k+1) < SPEED) [ ]
]

space(
  int r
  while ( (r=r+1)< 20 [ ]
]

letter char c [
  pause
  int k
  while ( (k=k+1) < SPEED) pause
  if (c= ='a') [dot:dash]
  else if (c= ='b') [dash;dot;dot;dot]
  else if (c= ='c') [dash;dot;dash;dot]
  else if (c= ='d') [dash;dot;dot]
  else if (c= ='e') dot
  else if (c=  ='f') [dot;dot;dash;dot]
  else if (c= ='g') [dash;dash;dot]
  else if (c= ='h') [dot;dot;dot;dot]
  else if (c= ='i') [dot;dot]
  else if (c= ='j') [dot;dash;dash;dash]
  else if (c= ='k') [dash;dot;dash]
  else if (c= ='l') [dot;dash;dot;dot]
  else if (c= ='m') [dash;dash]
  else if (c= ='n') [dash;dot]
```

```
        else if (c = = 'o') [dash;dash;dash]
        else if (c = = 'p') [dot;dash;dash;dot]
        else if (c = = 'q') [dash;dash;dot;dash]
        else if (c = = 'r') [dot;dash;dot]
        else if (c = = 's') [dot;dot;dot]
        else if (c = = 't') dash
        else if (c = = "u') [dot;dot;dash]
        else if (c = = 'y') [dot;dot;dot;dash]
        else if (c = = 'w') [dot;dash;dash]
        else if (c = = 'x') [dash;dot;dot;dash]
        else if (c = = 'y') [dash;dot;dash;dash]
        else if (c = = 'z') [dash;dash;dot;dot]
        else if (c = = '   ') [pause;pause;pause]
    ]

    morse char s(0) [

        SPEED = 12

        while(s(0))[
            letter s(0)
            s = s + 1
        ]
]

practice [
    char c
    int k,n,r,rl
    ps"how many letters"
    k = gn
    ps"how many repeats"
    r = gn
    ps "speed"
    SPEED = gn
    ps "seed"
    seed = last = gn
    while ((n = n + 1)< = k) [
        c = random 'a','z'
        r1 = 0
        while ((r1 = r1 + 1)< = r) letter c
        letter ' '
        putchar c; putchar ' '
    ]
]
```

To run the program, first clear out the program buffer:

```
tc>.1
tc>.d 999
```

and then load the program:

```
tc>.r morse
1691
0 86 1691 10309
tc>
```

Now you can either

```
tc>.practice
```

or

```
tc>.morse
```

your way to code proficiency.

The tiny-c Programming Language

The examples in the last chapter gave you a hint of what tiny-c programming is like. You probably have a hundred, a thousand, yea verily five or six questions about exactly how to build tiny-c functions and programs. What are the rules for variable names? What kinds of numbers are available? How do I build expressions? What statements alter program flow? What functions are in the system library? How do I link program parts together? How do I get at peripherals?

In this chapter we will cover all the gritty details of the tiny-c programming language. Keep in mind that the details don't tell you how they are intended to be used. You learn this by studying tiny-c programs. You've already started doing this; we'll do it some more in Chapter 3. For now, let's go wrestle with the nits and the lice.

COMMENTS, CONSTANTS, AND VARIABLES

Programs in tiny-c are built from *comments, constants, variables, keywords*, and *punctuation*. In this section we cover the first three: comments, constants, and variables.

Comments

An important part of a tiny-c program doesn't affect how the program behaves at all! It does, however, influence how useful the program becomes and how long it remains useful. This strange part of tiny-c is the *comment.*

Comments are simply notes that you write to anyone who might read the program. They are totally ignored during the execution of the program. Even the very best programmers feel that they lose touch with their own code after they've been away from it for more than 6 months. So the person you are helping most is yourself.

Comments in tiny-c begin with /* and continue to the end of the line. Apostrophes ('), quotes (''), and brackets ([]) cannot be used in comments. Comments can contain any information whatsoever, e.g.,

```
total_tax = total_tax + state_tax /* The capital of Texas is Austin
```

but they are intended to explain what's really going on in the program at the point the comment is written. Comments such as

```
total_tax = total_tax + state_tax /* Add state tax to total tax
```

aren't very helpful even though they do pertain to the program. Something like

```
total_tax =total_tax + state_tax /* Section 345.17 of US Tax Code
```

tells you why you're doing what your doing and will help you figure out the program when you come back to it a year from now.

Names

Names of functions and variables can be one or more characters long. If more than 8 characters are used, only the first seven and the last are significant. The first character must be alphabetic, either upper- or lowercase. The rest must be letters, numbers, or underbars (_). Names cannot have embedded blanks. Upper- and lowercase letters are considered distinct, so

```
GUESS
guess
```

are different names. Furthermore, names may *not* begin with any of these character strings:

```
if
else
while
return
break
char
int
MC
```

These are the tiny-c keywords; their use is reserved for their special tiny-c meaning.

Get into the habit of using variable names to really name what they denote. We beat this horse pretty thoroughly in Chapter 1 but the suggestion bears repeating because it's one of the key differences between tiny-c and BASIC. There can be little confusion about what the variable **chapter_title** holds. Who knows what **A$** holds?

Constants and Variables

There are two kinds of data in tiny-c, *integers* and *characters*. A *constant* is a literal data value. It is a specific value of one of these kinds of data. For example,

7 is an integer constant

'a' is a character constant

Integer constants consist of a string of digits 0 through 9. Character constants consist of any ASCII character (except an apostrophe) between apostrophes.

A *variable* is a named cell that holds one datum value. A variable is created by declaring its name and the type of datum it can hold, before its first use in an executable statement. This is accomplished by an **int** or **char** statement. Pascal and FORTRAN, to name two other languages, also require declaration statements; unlike FORTRAN, however, there are no predeclared integer and real variable types in tiny-c. For example, the two statements

```
int width, length
char letter
```

declare the existence of three variables: two integer variables names **width** and **length**, and one character variable named **letter**. Each can hold one datum of its respective type. The declaration statement sets the value of integers to 0 and the value of characters to ASCII 0 (NUL).

Arrays and Array Elements

An *array* is a list of variables of the same type. The statements

```
int value(10)
char buffer(80)
```

declare an integer array, called **value** with 11 integer elements and a character array called **buffer**, with 81 character elements.

A particular array element is picked out using a *subscript*. For example,

```
value(7)
```

names element 7 in the array **value**. Every array has a zeroth element:

```
value(0)
```

and a last element:

```
value(10)
```

When you declare an array, you in effect give the name of its last element. Thus, **value** has eleven elements:

```
value(0), value(1), . . ., value(10)
```

The subscript of an array can be any expression.

```
value(i + 10 * k)
```

Even in a declaration, the subscript can be an expression. This is a convenient way of setting several arrays to the same or related sizes.

```
int size
size = 10; int row(size), column(size), matrix(size*size)
```

Note that **matrix** is *not* a two-dimensional array, but a single list of 101 elements. However, it can be addressed as a two-dimensional(0-9, 0-9) matrix this way:

```
int row, col
row = 7
col = 3
matrix(row + size * col) = . . .
```

Locals, Globals, and Arguments

A variable's *scope* is the program region over which the variable's name is recognized. Where a variable is declared determines its scope. There are three places a variable can be declared and therefore three scopes in a tiny-c program:

locals	Local variables are declared within the body of a function, i.e., inside the **[]** part of the function.
globals	Global variables are declared outside all functions.
arguments	Function argument variables are declared after a function name but before the **[** beginning the function body.

In the **guessnum** program, **guess**, **number**, and **range** are local variables. The first two, **guess** and **number**, are local to the function **guessnum**. The last one, **range**, is local to the function **random**. The variables **seed** and **last** are globals, as are the function names **guessnum** and **random**. The variables **little** and **big** are arguments.

Locals are created when a function is entered and destroyed when the function is exited. When they are created they are initially set to 0 or NUL. Global variables may be accessed by all functions and preserve their values between function calls. Function arguments are local variables which get their initial values from the calling function.

Within a function the following names can be used:

- Locals in the function.
- Arguments of the function.
- All globals in the program.
- All functions in the program.
- All system library functions and variables.

Technically, arguments are locals and function names are globals, so this rule is easier to remember as:

■ *A function can use its own locals and all globals.*

All the locals within a function must have different names. But two different functions can each have their own local variable named i, for example. The two versions of i are kept separate. All global names including function names must be different.

Duplicate names are not detected or diagnosed by the tiny-c interpreter. A program will execute but the second declaration of the name will be ignored. The first declared name is always used. One form of duplication is important, however: you can have a local and global variable of the same name, and they are kept separate. Within the function that has the local, the local name prevails. Elsewhere the global prevails.

ARRAYS AND POINTERS

A *pointer* is a memory address. A *pointer variable* is a variable whose *value* is a memory address. You have already discovered that

```
char x(3)
```

declares a list of four character variables. They have names x(0), x(1), x(2), and x(3). This statement also declares a pointer variable named x and initializes it with the address of x(0). It is easy to visualize this way:

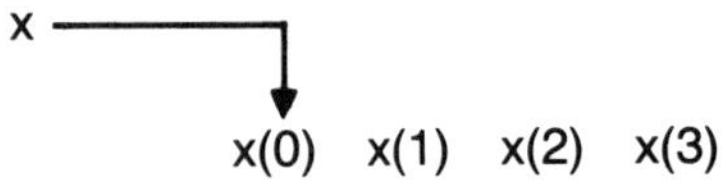

The arrow from x to x(0) indicates that the value in x is the address of x(0).

A *pointer expression* is a pointer plus or minus an integer expression. A pointer variable can be assigned a new value using a pointer expression. For example,

```
x = x + 1
```

adds 1 to x; since the size of things that x points to is 1, this results in:

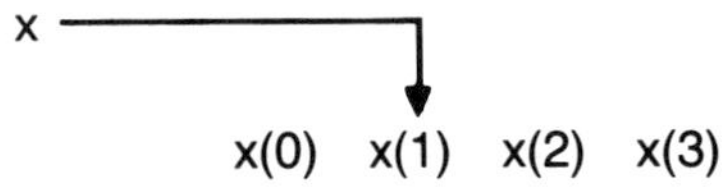

You have to be careful to keep track of the size of the things that pointer variables point to. The tiny-c language doesn't keep things clean for you like its big sister C does. For example, suppose we had declared

```
int y(3)
```

and then set

```
y = y + 1 /* BEWARE: y points to things of size 2
```

In this case y would *not* be pointing to the second element in the array, but instead would be pointing to the middle of the first element!

Ordinary arithmetic is done in tiny-c with pointer variables, not C's special kind of pointer arithmetic that takes into account the size of what is pointed to. If you wanted y to point to the second element in the array, what you should have done is set

```
y = y + 2 /* BETTER: y points to second element
```

Pointers can also be assigned to other pointers. The statements

```
char buffer(80), pointer(0)
pointer = buffer + 2
```

set up the following arrangement:

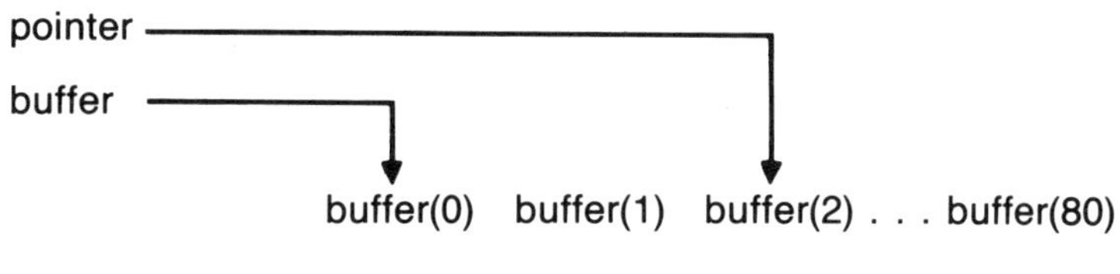

Character Strings Are Pointers Are Integers

A character string is a pointer to a character array initialized with the string and a null byte at the end. (Read that again just to make sure you got it.) Thus,

```
"cat"──┐
       ↓
      'c'  'a'  't'  0
```

This fact, coupled with the fact that pointers are just integers in the IBM PC version of tiny-c, lets us set up arrays of character strings:

```
int month(12)
month_initialize [

month(1)  = "January"
month(2)  = "February"
month(3)  = "March"
month(4)  = "April"
month(5)  = "May"
month(6)  = "June"
month(7)  = "July"
month(8)  = "August"
month(9)  = "September"
month(10) = "October"
month(11) = "November"
month(12) = "December"]
```

After calling **month_initialize**, a reference to **month(i)** produces a pointer to the character string naming month i. For example,

```
ps month(9)
```

prints "September."

Using Pointers to Peek and Poke

You can get at specific memory locations in the data segment of the PC's memory by using pointers. This is sometimes called *peeking* and *poking* after the BASIC functions that perform this service. If you enter

```
tc>.[int y(0);y = 4000;pn y(0)]
```

you will print out the value of the contents of memory location 4000 in the data segment of the PC's memory. Without any way of changing segments it isn't clear that this buys you much. But it does open up the following very useful possibility.

Using Pointers to Return Multiple Values

Pointers are frequently used as arguments of functions because they let a called function change variables local to the calling function, thus returning more than one result. The system library function **num** is a good example. It must return both the number of characters scanned and the value derived from those characters.

```
num char b(5);int v(0) [
```

```
    v(0) = 0
      ;
    v(0) = expression
      ;
    return k
]
```

The arguments to **num** are both pointers.

Here's an example of a call on **num**

```
int val(0)
m = num "17", val
```

Notice that the arguments "17" and **val** are both pointers. The argument **val** is the pointer that is being used to return a value to the calling function outside of the normal function value-returning machinery.

The standard rule for argument passing applies. Copies of the arguments' values are placed in the function's local variables. So we have

val
v
val(0) (which becomes v(0) within num)

The original argument, **val**, cannot be changed, but the word it points to can be. In fact, **v(0) = 0** has the effect of changing **val(0)**. The derived value is returned via the pointer **v**, and the number of characters scanned is returned as the value of the entire function **num**. In effect, a call on **num** says, "Here are the characters to examine and here is where to put the value of what you see."

Pointers are a way for one function to provide another function with the ability to change values of its local variables. This is useful when the called function has more than one thing to return to the calling function.

OPERATORS

The tiny-c operators described in Table 2-1 are used to do arithmetic, to compare values, and to assign values to variables. We will first take up their use in simple circumstances using one or two primaries. Then we consider more complex uses. Operators are the punctuation of expressions.

Uses of Assignment

The assignment operator = can be used anywhere a binary + or − can be used. For example,

```
array(k=k+1) = w-(x=y/z)
```

performs three assignments. The variable **x** is set to the value of **y/z**, and **k** is set to **k+1**. The new-value-of-**k** element of **array** is set to **w** minus the new value of **x**. Also consider

```
x = y = z = 0
```

Table 2-1. The tiny-c Operators.

Operator	Use	Definitions
unary +	+x	When used alone to the left of a variable, the plus sign is called a *unary plus*. It has no effect and is used sometimes for readability.
unary −	−x	When used alone to the left of a variable, the minus sign is called a *unary minus*. The value of −x is the negative of the value of x.
*	x*y	Multiplication. The value is multipled by y.
/	x/y	Division. The value is x divided by y. If there is a fraction, it is discarded; the result is an integer. So 7/2 is 3, and −7/2 is −3.
%	x%y[6]	Remainder. The value is the remainder of x/y. So 7%2 is 1, and −7%2 is −1.
+	x+y	Addition, also called *plus* or *binary plus*. The valve is the sum of x and y.
−	x−y	Subtraction, also called *minus* or *binary minus*. The value is the difference between x and y.
<	x<y	Less Than. The value is 1 if x is arithmetically less than y; otherwise it is 0.
>	x>y	Greater Than. The value is 1 if x is arithmetically greater than y; otherwise it is 0.
< =	x< = y	Less Than or Equal To. The value is 1 if x is less than or equal to y; otherwise it is 0.
> =	x> = y	Greater Than or Equal To. The value is 1 if x is arithmetically greater than or equal to y; otherwise it is 0.
= =	x = = y	Equal to. The value is 1 if x and y are equal; otherwise it is 0.
! =	x ! = y	Not Equal To. The value is 1 if x and y are not equal; otherwise it is 0.
=	x = y	Assignment. The value y is assigned to x. Then the expression x = y assumes the value of y.

Here **z** is set to 0. Then **y** is set to the value of **z=0**, that is, to 0. Then **x** is set to the value of **y=0**, also 0.

Order of Evaluation

When you write expressions with three or more primaries, the order of evaluation becomes important. For example, is

    9 + 6/3

equal to 5 or 11? Standard algebra conventions would do the division first, then the addition, so the answer is 11. The tiny-c interpreter works the same way. All the operators are assigned a *precedence*. In the absence of parentheses, the operators with the highest precedence are done first. Table 2-2 shows the order of precedence in tiny-c.

Table 2-2. Precedence of tiny-c Operators.

PRECEDENCE	OPERATORS
highest ⇕ lowest	unary + unary − * / % + − < > <= >= == != =

So the value of

    7+3 5 is (7+3) 5 is 0 (not 8)
    −1+7 is (−1)+7 is 6 (not −8)

Furthermore,

    x = 1+y = 2

is **x = (1+y) = 2** which is illegal because you may not set an expression **(1+y)** to anything.

However,

    x = 1+(y=2)

sets **y** to 2 and **x** to 3.

    x = 1+y == 2

is **x = ((1+y) == 2)**, which sets **x** to 1 if **1+y** is 2; otherwise it sets **x** to 0.

All the above cases are resolved by the precedence rule, but sometimes that is not enough. For example, is

    7 - 2 + 1

equal to 4 or 6? Standard algebra would say 6. Note that + and − have the same precedence, so we cannot use precedence to determine which goes first. The tiny-c convention is that the evaluation is done left-to-right. Thus,

    7-2+1 = (7-2)+1 = 6
    7/2*2 = (7/2)*2 = 6

(Remember that 7/2 is 3.) But what about this?

```
x = y = z = 0
```

Here is the exception. A series of assignments is done right-to-left.

Using Parentheses

Parentheses are used to change the order of performing operations. They take precedence over the rules of precedence. In our very first example, if the desired result was 5, you would write

```
(9+6)/3
```

An expression within parentheses is evaluated and then this value is used with the operator outside the parentheses. Within parentheses, precedence and grouping rules determine order. Therefore

22/(9+6/3) is 22/11 is 2 (not 4)

because the precedence rule says 9 + 6/3 is 11.

Understanding Computer Arithmetic

All computers have limits on how large a number can be handled. When the limits are exceeded the number is said to *overflow*. For the IBM PC and PCjr versions of tiny-c, the numbers must be in the range

$-32768 <= \text{number} <= 32767$

When a calculation would be outside this range, here is how to determine what happens. Subtract (or add if the calculation is too negative) 65,536 repeatedly from the result until it lies in the correct range. That is the answer. The example in Chapter 1 is

```
last    = last * seed
        = 9801 * 99
        = 970299
```

which is outside the range. Subtracting 65,536 fifteen times gives the value used by the computer:

```
        = 970299 - 15 * 65536

        = -12741
```

EXPRESSIONS

Expressions are formed from operators, parentheses, and primaries. They are used to calculate and store data and to invoke functions. *Primaries* designate the data to be

used in expressions and the destinations for results of expressions. They are the atomic elements of expressions. The six types of primaries in tiny-c are shown in Table 2-3.

Table 2-3. The tiny-c Primaries.

PRIMARIES	EXAMPLES
constants	10,'c'
strings	"hello"
variables	x, total
array variables	buffer (7)
array names	buffer
functions	pl, beep

An *integer constant* may be signed. Its value must be between −32768 and 32767 inclusive. An integer uses two bytes of storage. A *character constant* is always enclosed in apostrophes. A character uses one byte of storage.

Integers and characters are completely interchangeable in expressions. A character variable may be used as a one-byte integer whose value is in the range −128 to 127. This is occasionally useful, as in:

```
char newline, ch, digit
newline = 10 /* Puts an LF in newline.
ch = getchar
digit = ch - '0' /* Converts an ASCII digit to
/*  its integer value.
```

A character string constant is technically a two-byte constant which has as its value the address of the first element of an array of characters. Thus,

```
"hello"
```

is the address of the first element of an array of six characters initialized with 'h', 'e', 'l', 'l', 'o', and 0. Two-byte constants or variables, which may also be used as addresses, are called *pointers*. Thus, a character string is a pointer to its own first character.

A *subscript expression* may be an arbitrary expression. The smallest subscript is 0, the largest is the declared size of the array. If an array's subscript falls outside these bounds, a subscript error is recognized. An exception to this rule is when an array is declared to be of size 0. Any positive or negative subscript may be used; such an array can access, in effect, any element in the direct address space of the computer.

Since function names have values, they may be used in expressions as though they were variable names. The value of a function name is the value returned by the function when it is called. In the guessnum program, the use of the function name random in

```
number = random(1,100)
```

is an example of the use of a function name as a variable.

STATEMENTS

A *statement* is a basic unit of action in tiny-c. It is the atomic "Do it!" A simple statement ends with a semicolon (;), with the end of the line, or with the beginning of a comment. A left bracket ([) begins a compound statement. The matching right bracket (]) closes it. A right bracket also ends the immediately preceding simple statement.

There are only six tiny-c simple statements:

expression
if
if-else
while

```
return
break
```

Now you know how tiny-c got its name!

First we will define each of the statements and then we will talk about some idioms for using them.

The Expression Statement

An *expression* statement is the most frequently seen statement. When an expression is encountered it is simply evaluated, along with all associated assignments and function calls. For example,

```
ships__remaining = initial__fleet__size - sunk("Atlantic") - sunk("Pacific");
```

The If Statement

An **if** statement is called a *selection statement* because it selects whether or not another statement will be executed:

if (*expression*) *statement*

The *statement* part of an **if** statement is executed if and only if the value of the *expression* part is non-zero. The statement can be compound, as in:

```
if (error < 0) [
      pl "error negative; enter new value"
      target = 1000 + gn
]
```

The If-Else Statement

The **if-else** statement is another selection statement. This construction selects between two statements presented as follows:

if (*expression*) *statement__1* **else** *statement__2*

Statement__1 is executed if and only if the value of the expression is non-zero. Otherwise, *statement__2* is executed. Either may be compound. Whether compound or not, either statement can start on a new line. The **else** also can be on a separate line.

```
if(new__buffer = get__memory(512)) [
      new__buffer(0) = 511
      return new__buffer
] else [
      pl "Out of memory"
      return 0
]
```

The While Statement

The **while** statement is a *repetition statement* because it can cause another statement to be executed again and again. Here is the format:

while (*expression*) *statement*

The **while** statement works just like the **if** statement except that the statement part is done repeatedly until the value of the expression becomes zero. The statement is not evaluated at all if the expression is initially zero. As with **if** and **if-else**, the statement may be compound and can start on a new line.

```
while(change > epsilon) [
    new_value = iteration(old_value)
    change = absolute_value(new_value - old_value)
    old_value = new_value
]
```

The Return Statement

The **return** statement is called a *interruption statement* because it interrupts the normal sequential flow of program execution. It takes this form:

return *expression*

When a **return** is encountered, the function containing it halts at once. The value of the expression part of the return statement becomes the returned value of the function. The expression part is optional; if it is omitted, a zero is returned.

```
factorial(n) int n [
    if(n < 1)      return 0
    else if(n == 1) return 1
    else      return n*factorial(n-1)
]
```

The Break Statement

The **break** statement is another interruption statement. It interrupts a **while** loop rather than a function evaluation. When a **break** is encountered the innermost **while** is terminated immediately regardless of the value of its conditional expression. Control is transferred to the same point as if the **while** expression had evaluated to false.

```
while(1) [
    if(bored) break
    play_it_again_sam
]
/* Control comes here from the break
```

In tiny-c, **while(1)** is how you say "forever." The only way to exit from this loop is via the **break** statement.

Techniques for Using tiny-c Statements

The above paragraphs define the six tiny-c statements completely and can serve as a quick reference if you forget some detail of how a statement works. Here are some not-so-obvious but frequently used consequences of their definitions.

The if and **while** statements can be nested in any way. It is wise to use a consistent style of indenting when doing so.

```
while((i = i + 1) < 10)
        if(i%2)
        while((j = j + 1) < 10) odd_function(a(10*i + j))
        else
        while((j = j + 1) < 10) even_function(a(10*i + j))
```

Notice that no brackets are needed since the first **while** has a simple statement—the **if-else** statement—as its target; the **if** and the **if-else** have simple **while** statements as their targets. The expression in an **if**, **while**, or **return** statement, like any expression can invoke functions.

A frequently used technique is to get input from a user via one of the system library functions until end-of-input is signalled.

```
while(gs(input_buffer))
        process(input_buffer)
```

The system library function **gs** (get_a_string) gets a character string from the terminal and places it in the array supplied as its argument, **input_buffer** in this case; the **gs** library function returns the number of characters, excluding the NUL terminator character. If you just type a carriage return at **gs**, it will set **input_buffer(0)** equal to 0, return a value of 0, and cause the **while** to terminate.

The statement part of an if statement can also be another **if** statement, as in

```
if (x<10) if (x>7) y = 1
```

Since the second if statement is a simple statement, no brackets are necessary. The variable **y** is set equal to 1 when **x** is less than 10 and greater than 7.

We saw in the Morse code program that *statement_2* of an **if-else** can be another **if-else**, whose *statement_2* is another **if-else**, and so on. For example:

```
command [
        char c
        c = gc
        if      (c == 'p') print
        else if (c == 'd') delete
        else if (c == 'w') write
        else if (c == 'r') read
        else pl "must be p d w or r"
 ]
```

Each **else** always gets paired with the last **else**-less **if**.

No nested brackets are needed since the target of each **if** and **else** is a simple statement. An **if** followed by a series of **else-if** pairs, followed by an **else**, graphically displays an OR construct. One and only one alternative is executed.

Always keep in mind that anywhere you can write a statement, you can write either a compound statement or any of the six simple statements.

FUNCTIONS

A function can be used anywhere in an expression except to the left of an assignment. When a function is used in an expression, we say the function is *called.* When you call a function, it must be defined somewhere in your program, or be in the system library, or be the special function MC.

The Number of Arguments

Every function is defined with a specific number of arguments. The **random** function has two arguments, **little** and **big.**When a function is called, values must be supplied for each of the function's arguments. It is an error to supply too many or too few values. Thus, **random** must always be called with two arguments, the **ps** function must always be called with one, and **gn** must always becalled with none.

The argument values are written as a list of expressions separated by commas. The list, even if empty, can always be enclosed in parentheses, and sometimes must be. Arguments themselves may invoke functions. Arguments are evaluated left to right. Here are some legal calls on random.

```
random (1, 100)
random (gn (), gn())
random (k = random (-10,10), k+10)
```

Notice that each call to **random** has two arguments because **random** is defined with two arguments.

If an argument is an array, then the supplied value must be a pointer of the same data type. For example, the argument to the library function **pl** is a character array, so a character pointer is the only valid argument.

```
pl "hello"
```

is valid because "**hello**" is a pointer to a character array initialized with 'h', 'e', 'l', 'l', 'o', and 0.

If an argument is not an array, then any value can be supplied, but usually it will not be a pointer. Neither argument to **random** is an array, so the supplied values may be of any type.

```
random 1,100
```

returns a number between 1 and 100.

```
random 'a','z'
```

returns a random lowercase letter.

```
char array(100)
random array, array+100
```

returns a random address within **array**. Of course, this rule also applies to function definitions which are included in your tiny-c program. In the following example, the function **length** has one array argument and one non-array argument:

```
char array(10)
int k,l
k = length(array,l) /* array is a character pointer
     ,
     ,
     ,
]
length
char string(0)  /* string is a character pointer
int n        /* n is not an array
[
     ,
     ,
     ,
```

Parentheses

Parentheses around the argument list of a function are always allowed, but you can leave them off in certain cases. This is done primarily to make input/output functions a bit more legible. In the following forms, omitting parentheses around arguments is acceptable.

```
k = function arg, arg, arg
k = function
function arg, arg, arg
function
```

The general rule is:

- *If a function and its arguments are the last part of an expression, its parentheses may be omitted.*

Whenever the function is involved in a more complex expression, parentheses must be used. For example,

```
number = gn
```

is allowed, but gn in the expression

```
number = (gn( ) + 10)/2
```

needs the parentheses as shown.

There is no problem with complicated function arguments without parentheses, so this:

```
pn 142*x - y/17 + z%42
```

will print a number.

If the first argument begins with a left parenthesis, the argument list must be enclosed in parentheses. For example:

```
pn (7+2)/3
```

will be interpreted as follows:

a) The expression (7 + 2) is the argument to **pn** because of the **(**.
b) Call **pn**, which prints a **9**.
c) Function **pn** returns **0** as its value.
d) The expression **0/3** is evaluated and the result discarded.

This is probably not what was desired. Rewriting it as:

```
pn ((7 + 2)/3)
```

will print the value of 7 + 2 divided by 3.

Call by Value

When a function with arguments is invoked, the *value* of each argument is passed to the function. A local copy of the value is made within the function. The function can change the local copy, but this will not change the original. For example,

```
x = 10
blast x
pn x
    ,
    ,
    ,
blast int x [
x = 9999
]
```

The **pn** will print a 10. Function **blast** changes its local copy of **x** but not the original value. Notice that there are, in fact, two **x** variables: one local to the calling function and one local to the called function, **blast**. When **blast** is called, the second is created and initialized with the value of the first argument to **blast**—namely, the current value of the first **x**, 9999.

If you want to have a called function change a value in the calling function, then use an array of size one and pass the address of the array to the called function. A local copy of the *address* of the value will be produced in the called function; when the called function changes the contents stored at the address, it will be changing the value itself. For example,

```
calling__function [
    int local__variable(0)
    local__variable(0) = 7
    change__my__variable(local__variable)
    pn local__variable(0)
]
    change__my__variable int pointer(0) [
    pointer(0) = 2*pointer(0)
]
```

will cause 14 to be printed out by the pn statement in calling_function.

THE SYSTEM LIBRARY

The *system library* is a collection of 26 generally useful functions that are built into the tiny-c Shell. You have already made use of pl and gs, for example. These were system library functions.

Appendix C lists all the system library functions, together with a description of their use. These functions can be called freely by any function you write, or they may be called in a tiny-c Shell command. For example,

```
tc>.beep(523, 10)
```

will sound middle C for one second and

```
tc>.[int i,j;while(i=gn);j=j+i;pn j]
```

will add up a sequence of number entries terminated by 0.

In the chapter on the tiny-c Shell, we will discuss how you can add functions to the system library (or take functions away, for that matter). In this section we just want to elaborate on some of the more intricate aspects of a few of the system library functions.

Reading Characters from the Terminal

The system library has three functions to read characters from the terminal: the first two, getchar and gc, each read one character. Function getchar, the fundamental version, it behaves as follows:

1) Stops the program.
2) Waits for *one character* to be typed.
3) Starts up again.
4) Returns the character.

Function getchar is useful for one-letter commands.

Function gc reads more than one character, but only delivers the first letter it reads. It acts like this:

1) Stops the program.
2) Waits for a *while line* terminated by a carriage return to be typed.
3) Starts up again.
4) Returns the first character of the line.
5) Throws the rest of the line away.

This function works for answers to questions in a question-and-answer dialogue, or selecting entries in a list. A very common use is to test for the "y" of a "yes" answer:

```
ps "Do you want to play again?"
if (gc == 'y') [
play_again
]
```

Function gc gives you a little bit of robustness, since the user can type "y," or "yes," or "Yes, I'd really, really like to play again," and the program will land on its feed. (Of course, if they type, "Naturally I want to play again," you're out in the tall grass.)

The third function, gs, reads a character string. The function is defined as

```
gs char buffer(0)
```

so it must be called with a pointer to a character array as its argument. For example,

```
char input_line(80)
gs input_line
```

will read a character string from the console terminal into input__line(0), input__line(1), . . ., etc.

If you wrote

```
gs input__line + 10
```

the string would be read into input__line(10), input__line(11), . . ., etc. Note that a quoted string is really a pointer. That's why

```
ps "hello"
```

works. The last quote of the string is replaced by a null within tiny-c. You might like to wonder what

```
gs "hello"
```

will do.

Number Conversion

Pointers also are used in system library functions to return two or more results to the calling function. One example is num; it returns the number of characters scanned, but it changes the integer pointed to by its second argument. Thus, num should be called like this:

```
int v(0), k
k = num "17", v
```

There is no subscript on v in the call. This call will put 17 into v(0), and 2 into k.

Functions atoi and scann also use this method. The atoi function is just like num, except it handles a sign and leading blanks; num does *not* skip leading blanks.

String Comparison

The standard way to compare two character strings is with ceqn, since this type of comparison cannot be done with a tiny-c expression. For example, the following will *not* determine if "cat" has been entered at the console:

```
char input__line(10)
gs input__line
if (input__line == "cat") . . . /* WRONG !!!
```

The if will compare the address where input__line(O) is stored with the address where the 'c' of "cat" is stored, and will always be false. To test if "cat" has been entered, use ceqn:

```
char input__line(10)
gs input__line
if (ceqn(input__line, "cat", 3)) . . . /* RIGHT !!!
```

See Appendix C for another match function, ceq.

Scanning and Moving

The functions **movebl**, **countch**, and **scann** are written in C and therefore are quite fast. The **index** function is implemented partly in C and partly in tiny-c. Function **scann** is intended to scan quickly for the *n*th occurrence of a character in an array. Here's how to use it.

```
int n(0),
char x(100), where
n(0) = 7
where = scann(x, x+100, ' ',n)
```

This call to **scann** scans for the seventh blank in **x**. If there are seven or more blanks between **x** and **x + 100**, then **x + where** will point to the seventh, and **n(0)** will be zero when **scann** returns.

If there are fewer than seven blanks between **x** and **x+ 100**, then **where** will be 100 (The address relative to **x** of the last character examined) and **n(0)** will be seven minus the number of blanks in **x** when **scann** returns. Testing **n** is a convenient way to see why **scann** stopped.

```
if(n(0))
 less_than_seven_blanks
else
 found_seven_blanks
```

OTHER LIBRARIES

The **guessnum** program uses two functions from the *system library*, **pl** and **gn**. It also uses **random**, from the *optional library*. In Chapter 1 we suggested you build a set of useful, general-purpose functions, your own *personal library*. In Chapter 4 we will describe *machine calls* from which two additional librarys can be formed: *system machine calls* and *user machine calls*.

What is a library and what distinguishes one library from another?

A *library* is simply a collection of similar functions. Libraries differ from one another on the basis of what the functions contained within them have in common. *Frequency of use* and *common context of use* are two function similarities that are often used to establish libraries. The five libraries that have been mentioned so far could be briefly depicted as shown in Table 2-4.

The spirit of the system, optional, and system machine call libraries is that they have the same definition of each tiny-c installation, so that programs developed at one can be run at another. They are, in a sense, extensions of the tiny-c language.

The *system library* is a set of functions that is loaded with and used by the tiny-c Shell. As a result, these functions are accessible to all programs developed with the Shell. They need not be defined or specifically loaded to be used. They are described in detail in Appendix C.

The *optional library* is a set of tiny-c functions frequently useful to a programming project. Function **random** is one of these. They are not loaded with the Shell, so whenever they are used they must be specifically loaded. In principle, the optional library is a large collection of tiny-c program tools.

Table 2-4. The tiny-c Libraries.

LIBRARY	CONTENTS
system library	tiny-c functions used by the Shell and generally useful to all programs developed using the Shell.
optional library	tiny-c functions generally useful to tiny-c programs but not required frequently enough to be included in the system library.
personal library	tiny-c functions frequency used at a particular computer installation or by a specific class of application program.
system machine cells	Functions which are used so frequently by all tiny-c programs that they have been implemented in machine language to improve processing speed.
user machine calls	Functions which are so frequently used by tiny-c programs at a particular computer installation or by a specific class of application programs that they have been implemented in machine language to improve processing speed.

Your *personal library* is your own extention to the optional library.

Machine calls—both system and user—are coded in machine language. There is a set furnished with tiny-c (Appendix D) and you can build your own (Chapter 4). These are used for speed or to interface with special input/output devices.

Machine calls have an awkward, undescriptive syntax. For example, it isn't immediately obvious what

```
MC(47, 64, 1, 1001)
```

means or does. It is customary to wrap a machine call up with a nice name, like this:

```
plot int r, c, nf [
  return MC(r, c, nf, 1001)
]
```

Now you can write programs that say

```
plot(47, 64, 1)
```

and, although we haven't defined the **plot** function yet, "plot" is certainly somewhat more suggestive of what it does than "MC 1001."

Every addition to a machine call library therefore should be accompanied by an entry in one of the tiny-c libraries. You would place **MC 1001** in the user machine call library, and **plot** would be placed in either the optional or personal library of tiny-c functions.

The tiny-c Shell

The tiny-c Shell is a tiny-c program that lets you enter, edit, run, debug, save, and restore tiny-c programs. It consists of 13 global variables, a 30-line main program and 18 tiny-c functions totalling another 200 lines. You can study the Shell in Appendix E as a nontrivial example of tiny-c programming. Once you've understood it, you can change it to suit your own tastes and habits.

INITIAL PROGRAM LOAD

When you start the tiny-c program by typing

```
A>tinyc
```

the first thing the tiny-c program does is read the file TINYC.IPL into the interpreter's program buffer. The interpreter's program buffer is to the interpreter what the Shell's program buffer is to the Shell: it is where the tiny-c program that is being executed is held. The interpreter *links* the program text and starts execution at the first character of the buffer, that is, at the first character in the TINYC.IPL file. Linking is simply a process of giving the program text a once-over to find out where everything is.

The first set of global symbols that the link step encounters—all global symbols between the beginning of TINYC.IPL and the first end library statement—become the system library. Therefore, the typical structure of a TINYC.IPL file is:

system library functions and system global variables
endlibrary
level zero application program

The level zero application program is usually a command interpreting program of some kind, but it could be any tiny-c program. The only difference between a level zero application program and a one, two, or three application program is that when the main program of the level zero program returns or ends, tiny-c exits and control is returned to DOS.

You can read the section in Chapter 4 on linking and invoking tiny-c programs for more information on levels of application programs.)

When you prepare your own IPL program—by writing one from scratch or by simply modifying a copy of TINYC.IPL—you can name it TINYC.IPL so that tiny-c will load it automatically. Better (at least during development) is to ask tiny-c to load your IPL program instead of the default one. You can do that by adding its file name to the tiny-c startup command line:

```
A>tinyc newshell.ipl
```

This will cause tiny-c to load the file NEWSHELL.IPL rather than the default TINYC.IPL when it starts.

If the IPL program is not going to invoke other tiny-c programs then there is no use for a system library. In this case, the IPL program can simply be a tiny-c program that starts with a call to one of the functions in the program:

```
[hardwired_program( );]
hardwired_program [
,
,
,

]
```

In this case, tiny-c *becomes* hardwired_program. When this program ends, tiny-c ends and control is returned to DOS.

SQUEEZING A tiny-c PROGRAM

Because the tiny-c interpreter runs right off the program text, it takes longer for it to recognize a name like get_a_string than it does the name gs. Since we are very interested in making the level zero application—the tiny-c Shell in this case—run as quickly as possible, once we had it running using long names, we squeezed all the long and descriptive names down to unique two-letter names. This made the Shell run a bit faster.

It would be nice to have a tiny-c utility program that squeezed tiny-c programs. It would be even nicer to have tiny-c do it automatically when it linked a program. If your interests lay in hot-rodding tiny-c, finding a more efficient way of handling variable names is certainly a place to start.

CHANGING THE SYSTEM LIBRARY

The system library is nothing more than all the global symbols—variables and functions—from the beginning of the IPL file up to the first endlibary statement. In order to add a function to the system library, you simply include it in this section of code in the TINYC.IPL file. Now what could be easier?

Adding a System Library Function

For example, after I added the machine call to sound the beeper on the IBM PC and PCjr, I decided that this was a useful enough function to be included in the system library. Therefore, I stuck a function called **beep** in the system library section of TINYC.IPL so that I wouldn't have to remember the machine call number. You can see that, just before the **endlibrary** statement, I inserted the code:

```
beep int f,d
[MC f,d,17]
```

In the Shell program or in any application program I can now write

```
beep(freq, duration)
```

to get a beep of frequency **freq** for **duration** tenths of a second.

System Variables

The standard system library contains no global variables; it contains only functions. If the Shell wanted to talk directly with an application program or an application program had need to communicate back to the Shell, then it would have to do so using a global variable in the system library.

The user's name comes to mind as something that the Shell might ask the user when it started up and then make available to application programs via a system variable. All you would have to do is define a system variable such as

```
char sys_name(30)
```

in the system library area. You could then modify the Shell's BOOT program to read:

```
[pl "Enter user handle:"
gs sys_name; main;]
```

This would initialize sys_name for tiny-c, just as DOS has you initialize the date and time when it starts. One idea for using **sys_name** would be to customize the tiny-c prompt:

```
pl "Now what, ";ps sys_name
ps ">"
```

Changing System Library Functions

Since tiny-c, like C, has no built-in input/output or string handling functions, the system library functions are more a part of the language than they would be in richer languages such as FORTAN or COBOL. This means that the system library associated with tiny-c or C is a bigger factor in moving programs from one computer installation to another than it is with these other languages.

If, for example, you changed **gs** to be generate_a_symbol rather than get_a_string, a tiny-c program you got from a friend, thinking it was using a standard system service to get a string from the user, probably wouldn't be prepared to figure out what it was getting back when it called **gs**. Of course, if your tiny-c system is going to be running only programs you have written, then by all means set up the system library to be exactly what suits you best. But if you want to run other people's programs, or you want them to be able to run yours, it's a better idea to add new functions than to change the standard ones.

THE SHELL PROGRAM

One of the primary advantages of modular program design is that you can see what is happening at each and every level of detail in the program. This makes the program easier to understand and thus easier to improve.

Here is a high-level description of the tiny-c Shell program: Listing 3-1 shows what this main loop looks like in tiny-c:

Listing 3-1. Main loop for the tiny-c Shell.

```
while(1) [
ps"tc>"
  while ((line=gs(line))= =0) [ ] /*Read non-empty line.
  c=line(0)
  if (c= = '.') [ /* if it starts with a . then do it now
    if (num(line+1,val))goto(val) /*.number
    else if ((line(2)= =0) + (alpha(line(2))= =0)) [
      c=line(1)
      if  (c= ='p')print
      else if (c= ='d')dlines
      else if (c= ='l')locline
      else if (c= ='c')change
      else if (c= ='/')facts
      else if (c= ='r')progin
      else if (c= ='w')progout
      else if (c= ='x')return
      else [ps"???";pl" "]
    ] else start
  ]
  else if (c= ='-')up
  else if (c= ='+')down
  else insert
```

You've probably used the Shell enough by now to have some good ideas on how to improve it. Maybe there's a command that doesn't behave exactly as you'd like it to. Or maybe you have an idea for a new command. Take a few minutes and study the description of the loop, the code for the loop, and Table 3-1, which associates commands and handler functions. Just get the lay of the land. You'll pick up the details as you begin your Shell customization work.

Can you see how easy it's going to be for you to improve the tiny-c Shell? Here's a test. How you would go about making a lone carriage return mean +1? There's one way of doing it which only takes a one-line addition to main .

Adding A New Edit Command

A slightly more ambitious undertaking would be to add a new edit command, say z . First you have to add the statement

```
else if(c= ='z') z__command__handler
```

Table 3-1. Shell Command and Handler Functions.

STRING	CLASSIFICATION	HANDLER FUNCTION
.p	Edit Command	print
.d	Edit Command	delete
.l	Edit Command	locline
.c	Edit Command	charge
./	Edit Command	facts
.r	Edit Command	progin
.w	Edit Command	progout
.x	Edit Command	none . . . just return!
.letters	Statement	start
−	Cursor Movement	up
+	Cursor Movement	down
text	Program Text	insert

Table 3-2. Shell Global Variables.

VARIABLE	FUNCTION
pr	The program buffer: holds the lines of program text entered by the Shell's user.
lpr	The total length of pr.
lastline	The line number of the last line in pr.
progend	A pointer to the last character of program text in the pr buffer.
lineno	The current line number.
cursor	A pointer to the current line of program text in the pr buffer.
line	The array of user-input characters.
lline	The number of user-input characters.
ltext	The text being searched for.
len	The number of characters in ltext.

Table 3-2 (continued).

totext	The text to which the found text is being changed.
tolen	The number of characters in totext.
err	The error, if any, generated by running the program in pr.

to the edit command recognition statements in the main function. Then you have to add a z__command__handler function to the to the Shell program. That's all!

If your z command can have arguments, then the z__command__handler function will be responsible for processing the third and following characters in the user-entered string—the characters in line(2) , line(3), etc.—to find out if any arguments have been provided and, if so, what they are.

The State of the Shell

The 13 global variables in the Shell program (Table 3-2) describe the current state of the Shell. The state described by these variables should match exactly with perception notion of the current state the Shell's user holds in mind. The global variable cursor, for example, points to the current line in the program text buffer. This line should be the same as the line that the user thinks is the current line.

If your z command changes the current state, then the documentation for the z command will change the state in the user's mind and the code in the z__command__handler function will change the state as described by the 13 global variables. Make sure that what the documentation does to the user's mind is exactly what the z__command__handler does to the 13 variables.

Besides changing the current state, it is quite possible that your z command will expand the state of the Shell and the notion of the current state of the Shell that is in the user's head. For example, the z command might mark a particular line in the program but move cursor, the keeper of the current line, somewhere else. The pointer to the marked line would become a new global variable in the Shell program, and the notion of which line is currently marked would be added to the idea of the current state of the Shell in the user's mind.

4

The tiny-c Interpreter

There is only one wholly honest form of documentation for a computer program: the source code of the program itself. Anything else is mixed with the hopes, fears, dreams, wishes, and grand plans of the programmer. This, among other reasons, is why the tiny-c package includes the source code of the tiny-c Interpreter. If you ever have a question—and you will—that the documentation doesn't answer clearly, you can always, in the words of Reid Smith, "Go to the code." It, and only, it is the final arbiter of what is and isn't allowed.

Here are some facts about the IBM PC and PCjr version of the tiny-c Interpreter. It consists of

- 11 source files
- 18 global variables
- 38 functions
- 1446 lines of C
- 2220 bytes of data
- 19,249 bytes of executable code

The interpreter was compiled with the DeSmet C compiler and relies in no small part on the runtime library available with that product. If tiny-c sparks your interest in C, this compiler, together with its source code debugger, is an excellent starting point and a remarkable bargain.

In the narrative parts of this chapter we describe the action of each interpreter function. Besides the name of the function, each description includes arguments, results, and errors. The paragraph immediately following describes the action of the function.

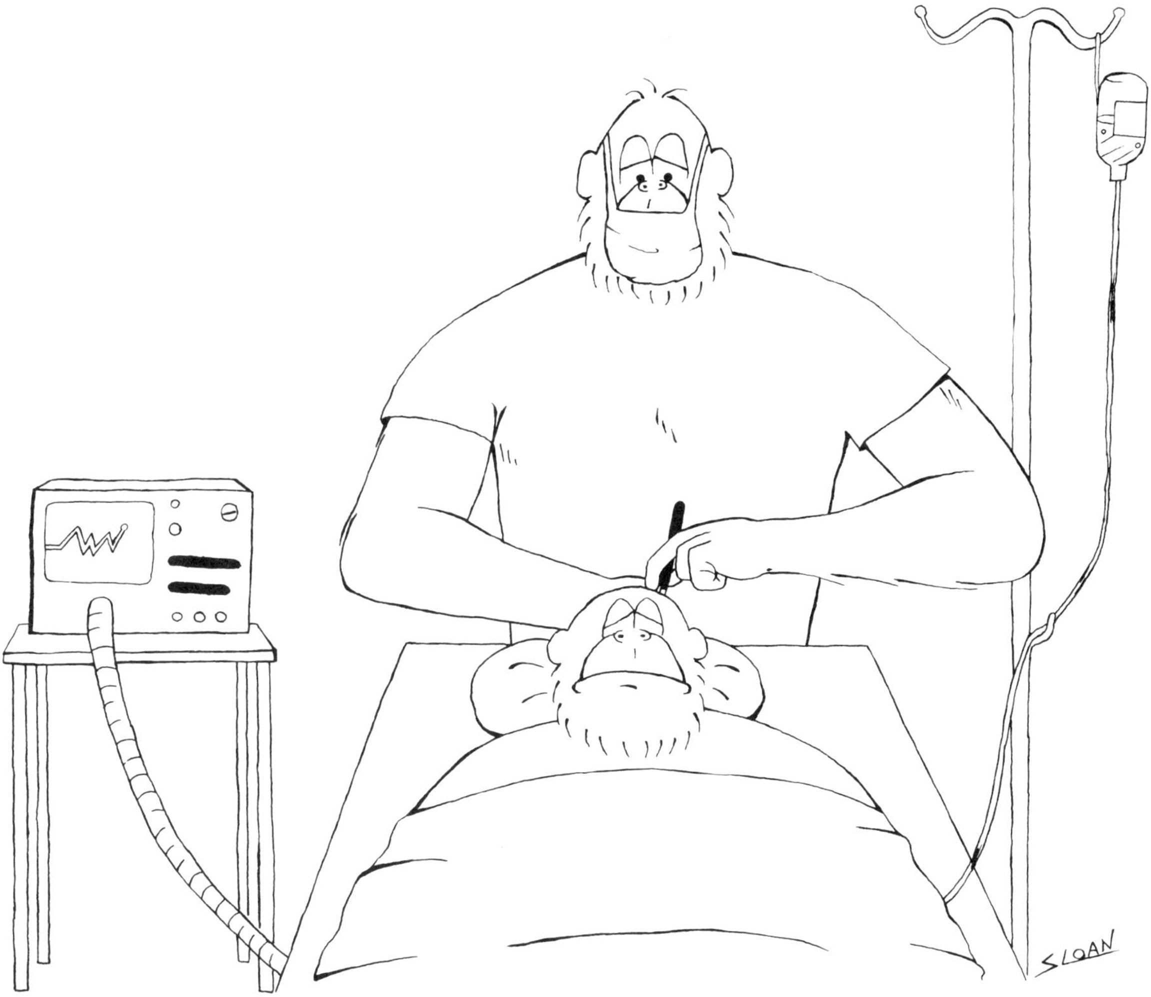

Arguments describe data given to the subroutine through its calling sequence, e.g., via registers or the machine stack. We do not say in the narrative how arguments are passed, because that varies among different implementations. Some routines will also use data in global cells such as **cursor** and **progend**. These are not listed as arguments. Their use is described under the action part of the narrative.

Results are data given back to the calling routine. This does not include modifications to the global cells. Many routines return no results to the calling routine. This does not mean they don't do anything! Don't confuse results (an explicit signal to the calling routine) with action (what the called routine does).

Errors refers to errors detected by the interpreter in the tiny-c program being processed. All errors result in a call to the **error** function. Many routines detect no errors.

Action describes what the routine accomplishes.

The narrative has been kept general, so it will apply to all implementations, even improved ones. For example, a faster search algorithm could be installed in **addrval**, but the narrative describing describing **addrval** should remain the same. The way we accomplish this is to say *what* **addrval** does, *not* how it does it. The "what-not-how" approach to software description assumes the reader can read listings to determine the explicit algorithm used.

GLOBALS, DATA OBJECTS, AND SIZING CONSTANTS

Before we get to describing the functions themselves, we will spend some time talking about the information milieu in which these functions operate. This milieu consists of global variables and data objects that the functions operate on, as well as system generation constants that determine the capacity of the tiny-c Interpreter.

Global Variables

There are 18 global variables which determine the overall state of the tiny-c Interpreter. These variables are referred to so frequently by interpreter functions that it makes more sense to make them universally available than to be constantly passing them around from function to function. The 18 global variables are defined in the next few paragraphs.

pr—A character array that holds all tiny-c being interpreted, together with the values for all currently allocated variables. For example, if a tiny-c program defines a global integer array of 100 values, the 200 bytes of storage needed to hold these 100 values are allocated in the **pr** array.

cursor—A character pointer that points into the **pr** array; the character pointed to by **cursor** will be the next character interpreted by the tiny-c Interpreter. In effect, **cursor** says where the interpreter is at any given instant.

fname—A character pointer into the **pr** array; it points to the first character of the variable or function currently being evaluated by the interpreter.

lname—A character pointer into the **pr** array; it points the last character of the variable or function currently being evaluated by the interpreter.

errat—A character pointer into the **pr** array; when an error is detected in interpretation, **errat** is set equal to **cursor** when the error was detected.

progend—A pointer into the **pr** array; points to the last tiny-c text character of the current tiny-c program. The value of **cursor** cannot go beyond **progend**.

prused—A pointer into the **pr** array; points to the last byte used in the array for text and value storage. The value of **prused** may not go beyond the end of the **pr** array. Program text goes from the beginning of **pr** to **progend**, and variable values go from **progend** to **prused**.

leave—A Boolean variable which is set to YES when a return statement is encountered; it acts like a break statement to terminate **while** loops and compound statements.

brake—A Boolean variable which is set to YES when break statement is encountered; it is used to terminate **while** loops.

err—A non-negative integer which is set to a tiny-c error code when an error in the interpretation of the tiny-c program text is encountered.

applvl—A nonnegative integer which holds the current application level (see Chapter 4 for more information on application levels.)

stackb—A pointer to item structures. It is the base of the tiny-c value stack.

top—A pointer into the tiny-c value stack, hence a pointer to item structures. It is the top of the tiny-c value stack.

varb—A pointer to variable structures; the base of the variable table.

nxtvar—A pointer to variable structures; contains the next free entry in the variable table.

funb—A pointer to function structures; represents the base of the function table and the descriptor of the system library level in the variable table.

curglobal—A pointer into the function table, hence a pointer to function structures; it is the descriptor of the global variables and functions in the current application program.

curfun—A pointer into the function table, hence a pointer to function structures; it is the descriptor of the local variables in the function currently being interpreted.

Data Objects

There are two data declarations in tiny-c, int and char. They declare data objects which have five intrinsic properties: name, class, size of one datum, length, address where allocated.

Name. The name of an object is given in its declaration. For example, in

```
int x(10)
```

the object has name x. At most, eight characters of a name are remembered, the first seven and the last. Longer names may be used, but their eighth through next-to-last characters mean nothing. (See the VLEN sizing constant below if you want to change this rule.) Thus

```
whathappened
whathapd
whathaphazard
```

all appear to tiny-c as the same name. The second of these is the canonicalized eight-byte form.

Class. There is a difference between x and y in:

```
char x, y(0)
```

Here x is a character datum, while y is the *address* of a character datum.

The number of addresses one must go through to get an actual datum is the *class* of the object, so x has class 0 and y has class 1. You can think of class as the "dimension" of the object when viewed as a matrix. Thus, x has dimension 0, and y dimension 1.

The address y(0) also has a class attribute; it is a character datum, so it has class 0. Consider

```
int vector(80)
```

Here **vector** has class 1, while **vector(17)** has class 0. Classes greater than 1 theoretically exist but are not implemented in tiny-c.

Size. *Size* refers to the size of the ultimately referenced object; it does not refer to the size of an array. All character data has size 1. All integer data has size 2. Thus, in

```
char letter, line(80)
```

both **letter** and **line** have size 1. If you added floating point numbers to tiny-c, their size would be 4 or 8.

Length. The *length* of an object is measured in number of data items, not bytes. All class O objects had length 1. Class 1 objects have lengths equal to the declared size of the array. Note that this is one larger than the number written, because element O must be counted. Thus,

```
char line(80)
int vector(80)
```

both have length 81.

Address. The *address* of an object is the lowest memory byte address where the object's value(s) is/are stored. An **n** byte object (where **n = size * length**) has its value(s) stored in **address, address + 1, . . ., address + n − 1.**

Sizing Constants

In the TC.H file you will find five *sizing constants* for the tiny-c Interpreter. These are values which determine the capacity or boundaries of the capabilities of the program. There is nothing particularly magical about the values used. If you find yourself running out of one resource or another, just change the value of the sizing constant and recompile and relink the interpreter. (Of course, you'll need a C compiler to perform this task.)

MAXSTACK. This constant establishes the maximum size of the value stack. Each value the interpreter computes that it cannot immediately use is pushed onto the value stack. For example, in 3*(4 + 7) the interpreter would push the 3 and the 4 on the stack until it evaluated 7, which it would also push onto the stack. When the interpreter finished with the 7, it would pop both the 7 and the 4 off the stack and push their sum, 11. Having completed the processing of the second term of the multiplication, it would pop the 11 and the 3, multiply them, and push the result, 33. Three units of the value stack would have been used in this process. The sizing constant **MAXSTACK** is set initially to 30. Unless you are writing very, very large complicated expressions, this should be sufficient.

MAXVAR. This sets the maximum number of active names. All functions and all global variables at all application program levels are always active. For the stock version of tiny-c this includes the system library functions, the tiny-c Shell functions and globals, and all functions written by the user. It also includes all the locals in all currently active functions. A function is active if it has been called but has not yet returned.

Constant **MAXVAR** is initially set to 200. There are 29 system library functions, 13 global variables, and 19 functions in the Shell, so the variable name space is about 30 percent full when you begin.

MAXFUN. The MAXFUN constant sets the maximum number of active functions. A function is *active* if has been called but has not yet returned. Each recursive instance of a function counts as another active function. The constant **MAXFUN** sets a limit (initially 30) on the length or depth of function calling chains.

MAXPR. The size in characters of the tiny-c program buffer is set by MAXPR. The program buffer in which you enter text when you use the tiny-c Shell is actually an array in the level zero tiny-c Shell program. This array, as well as the system library functions, the Shell program text, the other Shell global variables, are all held in tiny-c's internal program buffer. MAXPR determines the size of this mother of all program buffers.

This constant is set initially to 20,000. The system library and the tiny-c Shell comprise about 5,400 bytes and the Shell allocates roughly 12,300 bytes of global space, so the internal program buffer is about 90 percent full. Functions you enter into the Shell, together with space for their variable values, come out of the 12,000-character global program buffer allocated by the Shell and included in the above figures. This Shell program buffer could be increased to about 14,000 bytes before you'd have to increase the size of the internal program buffer.

VLEN. This sets the number of characters in a unique name. You recall that tiny-c names are unique up to the first seven letters and the last letter. This uniqueness was determined by the VLEN sizing constant. Its initial value is 8. If you wanted names to be unique up to the first n letters and the last one, set VLEN to n+1. Since the canonicalized version of the variable name is kept in the variable table, changing this sizing constant will also change the overall size of the variable table.

STACKS, TABLES, AND DATA STRUCTURES

There are five data spaces in the tiny-c Interpreter:

pr	The program buffer, which holds tiny-c program text *and* variables values (including all array elements).
stackb	The tiny-c value stack, which holds partial results in expression evaluations.
varb	The variable table, which holds the description but *not* the value of each variable and function name.
funb	The function table, which holds pointers into the variable table which define the scope of variable names.

In this section we will describe each of these data spaces in detail and document the functions used for their care and feeding.

The Variable Table

All functions and all currently active variables are described in the variable table. An entry in the variable table consists of 14 bytes:

0-7	Canonicalized eight-byte name.
8	Class.

9	Size of one datum.
10-11	Length in data elements.
12-13	Address of first value.

A class value of E means the entry represents a function name. Size and length are ignored in this case. The address value is where the cursor must be placed to begin execution of the function.

Currently active variables are:

- All library symbols, including system library functions.
- All global symbols, including functions.
- All local variables for active functions, including function arguments.

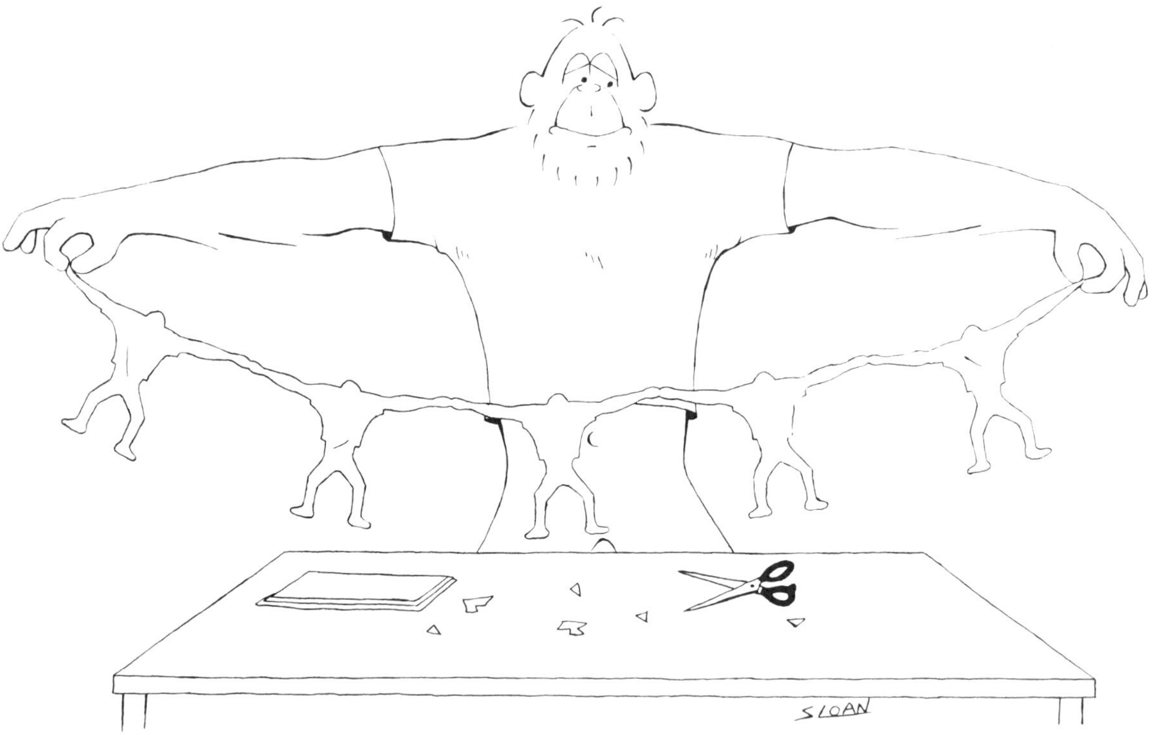

Remember a function is *active* if it has been invoked but has not completed. In the case of recursion, each incarnation counts as an active function. All function names are either global or library, and all are entered in the variable table. Note that the function's name is entered without regard for its active or inactive status. The active function simply determines which local variables are currently active.

Suppose the code shown in Listing 4-1 is being interpreted and control is currently in **function_1**.

Listing 4-1. Program fragment illustrating the role of the variable table in executing tiny-c functions.

```
  char global____symbol
main [
    int local__symbol
    function__1 (2, 3)
    function__2
]
function__1 int x,y [
    int n
      .
      . <------ statement currently executing
      .
]
  function__2 [
    char another__symbol
      .
      .
      .
```

The global symbols are:

global__symbol
main
function__1
function__2

The active functions are **main** and **function__1**. Their local variables are:

local__symbol
x
y
n

These eight variables—the four globals and the four locals—are the ones allocated in the variable table. Later when **function__1** returns, **x**, **y** and **n** are deallocated. When **function__2** is invoked, **another__symbol** is allocated. At this point six symbols are in the table:

global__symbol
main
function__1
function__2
local__symbol
another__symbol

The variable table is organized into layers so only those symbols accessible to a function will be searched. A symbol is accessible if it is

- Local to the function.
- Global to the program.
- In the system library.

This excludes variables local to active functions not currently executing. Thus, in Listing 4-2, the variables g and z are accessible to function_2; x and y, although active, are not accessible to function_2.

Listing 4-2. Program fragment illustrating the handling of local variables during function execution.

```
    int g
  main [
        int x
        function_1
  ]
  function_1 [
        int y
        function_2
  ]
  function_2 [
      int z
        .
        . <------ currently executing statement
        .
```

Layer 0 is reserved for system library symbols; function names and system-wide global variables, if any. Program globals are in layer 1 initially, but can occur in other layers. After layer 1, if there are n currently active functions, i.e. a main program, a function invoked by main, a function invoked by that function, etc., n levels deep, then those n functions are in layers 2, 3, . . ., n + 1. The locals for main are in layer 2. The locals for the currently executing function are in layer n + 1. This layer is pointed to by the interpreter global variable curfun.

When a symbol is needed, a systematic hunt for it is carried out. First, all symbols in the curfun layer are searched. If it isn't found there, then all symbols in the global layer are searched. If it isn't found there, then all symbols in the library layer are searched last. If it isn't found there, a symbol error is raised. Notice this order of search guarantees the properties in described in Chapter 2.

The Function Table

The mechanism for layering is the *function table*. An entry in the function table has four addresses.

0-1	The address of the first variable table entry for this function.
2-3	The address of the last variable table entry for this function.
4-5	The address of the variable table entry for the variable most recently used by this function.
6-7	The address in the program buffer of the value of the last variable entry for this function.

The address in **curfun** points to the first byte of the function table entry of the currently executing function. The address in **curglobal** points to the first byte of the function table entry for current globals.

Library symbols are always in layer 0, and **funb** points to the first byte of that layer. The implementation of the search order described above is simply to search symbols spanned by the function table entry pointed to by **curfun**, then the function table entry pointed to by **curglobal**, and finally the function table entry at **funb**.

Symbol Table Tools

The following functions manipulate and search the variable and function tables:

newfun
fundone
newvar
addrval

These subroutines use the auxiliary subroutine **canon** to canonicalize variable names to eight bytes. These five functions comprise the source file SYMBOL.C.

Function: newfun
Arguments: None
Results: None
Errors: Too many functions

Function **newfun** allocates a new layer in the function table, with zero entries in the variable table.

Function: fundone
Arguments: None
Results: None
Errors: None

Function **fundone** deallocates a layer in the function table, deallocates all variables in that layer, and deallocates all value space seized within that layer.

Function: newvar
Arguments: Canonicalized variable name, class, size, length, and value.

Results:	Address of first byte of allocated space.
Errors:	Too many variables or too many values.

Function **newvar** enters a new variable in the current layer of the variable table.

There are several considerations in allocating a value for a variable. If the variable is local or global, space is allocated and set to 0. If the variable is an argument to a function, and is class 0 (i.e. a single datum, not an array name) then space is allocated, and the passed value copied into the space. If the variable is an argument of a function, and is class greater than zero, then it is the address of an existing array. Space is not reallocated for these variables. The passed value—the array address—is entered as the new variable's address-of-first-value (bytes 12-13 of the variable table). Thus, in effect, the array is passed.

Values are allocated in the program buffer. The global variable **progend** points to the last byte used for program text, and the global variable **prused** points to the last byte used for program text and variables values.

Function:	addrval
Arguments:	Canonicalized variable name.
Results:	Address of first byte of allocated space, class, size, and length.
Errors:	Variable name not found.

Function **addrval** searches for the variable name and returns its properties. Searches locals, globals, and system library symbols in that order.

Function:	canon
Arguments:	Addresses of first and last bytes of an uncanonicalized variable name and the address of an eight-byte buffer.
Results:	Canonicalized variable name in buffer.
Errors:	None

Eight bytes are placed in the buffer. If the character string is shorter than eight bytes, it is padded on the right with nulls. If the variable name is longer than eight bytes, the first seven bytes and the last byte are placed in the buffer.

The tiny-c Stack

To evaluage expressions, tiny-c has a stack implemented in software, not to be confused with the 8088 machine stack. An entry on the tiny-c stack consists of five bytes:

0	class
1	lvalue
2	size
4-5	stuff

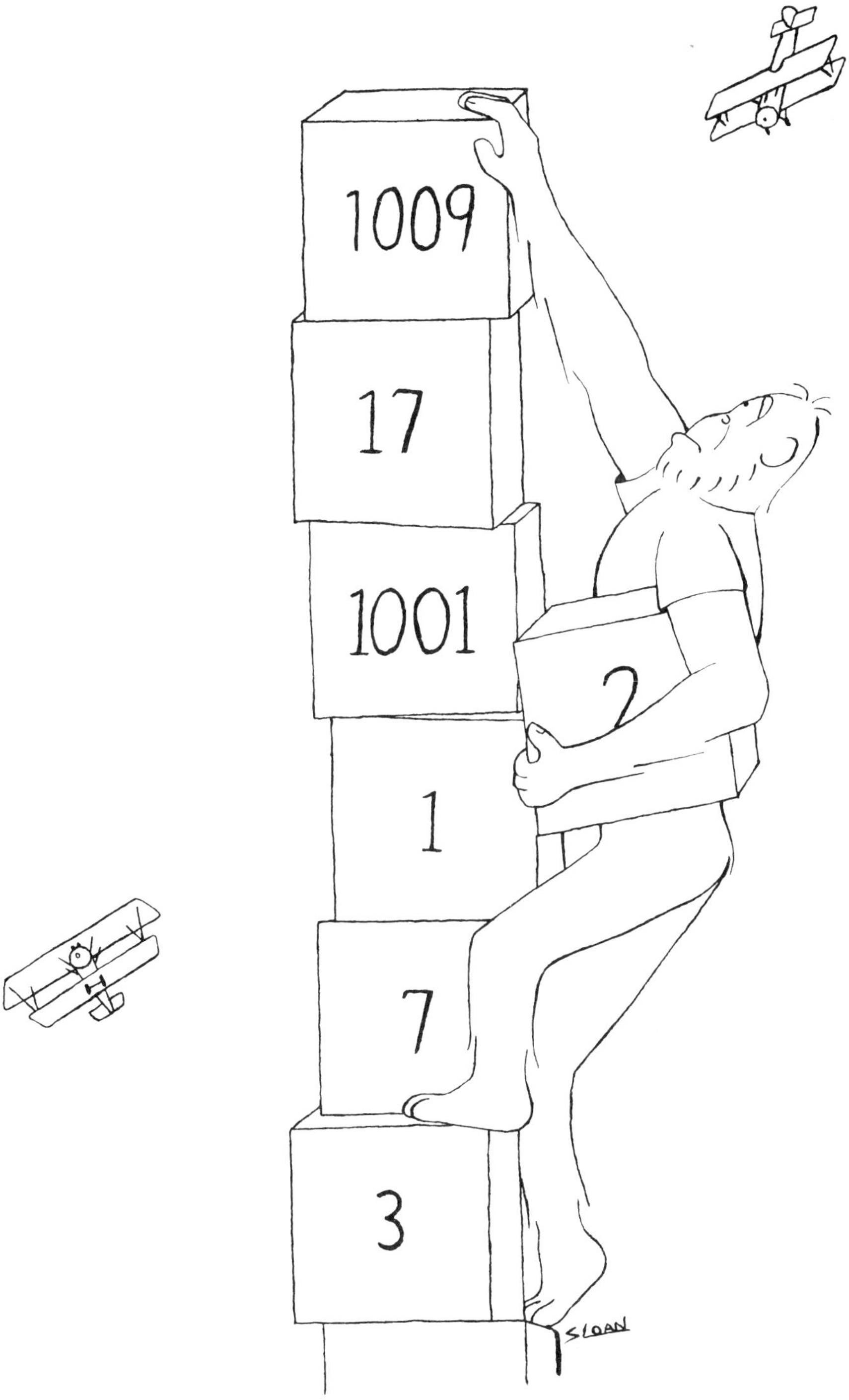
1009
17
1001
2
1
7
3
SLOAN

An **lvalue** *(left-side-value)* is any symbol that can be written to the left of an equal sign. Allowable lvalues include variable names, subscripted array names, and unsubscripted array names. The variable names and subscripted array names have class 0, and their value is a single character or integer datum. The unsubscripted array names have class 1 and their values are addresses.

Processing of an expression is done left-to-right. Whenever an **lvalue** is recognized, its attributes are put on the tiny-c stack. Bytes 4 and 5, **stuff**, are set to the address where the value is stored. An L is put in byte 1, **lvalue**, signifying **stuff** is a *reference* to the actual value. Whenever a constant is processed or the results of arithmetic must be stacked, the actual data value is put into **stuff**. An A is put into **lvalue**, signifying **stuff** *is* actual data.

Consider the processing of this expression:

```
K = J + 1
```

where K and J are both integers. Suppose K has address 4000, J has address 4002, and J has value 7. The tiny-c stack looks like Fig. 4-1.

tiny-c STACK

STEP	ELEMENT		CLASS	LVALUE	SIZE	STUFF
1	K	Top →	0	L	2	4000
2	J	Top →	0	L	2	4002
			0	L	2	4000
3	1	Top →	0	A	2	1
			0	L	2	4002
			0	L	2	4000

Fig. 4-1. Operation of the tiny-c stack in evaluating the expression K = J + 1.

At this point, the plus operation is performed. First, the 1 is popped off the stack. It is an actual value so it is left as a 1. Then the 4002 is popped. It is an **lvalue** so the contents of addresses 4002 and 4003 (two bytes because size is 2) are retrieved. This is the value of J, 7. They are added, and the sum pushed on the tiny-c stack as an actual (Fig. 4-2).

Now the equals operation is performed. The top entry, 8, is popped and held. The next entry is popped. It must be an **lvalue** but it is not converted to an actual because the current value of K is irrelevant. Only the address of K is needed, and that is 4000. The held 8 is stored in bytes 4000 and 4001, thus performing the assignment.

The value of the expression is 8. (Recall that all expressions, including those with an equal sign, have values.) So the last step in processing this expression is to push the 8 back on the stack as an actual (Fig. 4-3).

tiny-c STACK

STEP		CLASS	LVALUE	SIZE	STUFF
4	Top ——►	0	A	2	8
		0	L	2	4000

Fig. 4-2. The contents of addresses 4002 and 4003 are summed and pushed to the stack as an actual.

tiny-c STACK

STEP		CLASS	LVALUE	SIZE	STUFF
5	Top ——►	0	A	2	8

Fig. 4-3. The last step of the process: the value 8 is pushed back on the stack as an actual.

Stack Tools

The following subroutines manipulate the tiny-c stack:

push
pushint
pop
toptoi
eq

These five functions comprise the source code file STACK.C.

Function: push
Arguments: class, lvalue, size, stuff
Results: None
Errors: Stack full

The push function causes the arguments to be pushed onto the stack as its top entry.

Function: pushint
Arguments: stuff
Results: None
Errors: Stack full

Stuff is pushed onto the stack with class 0, lvalue A, size 2.

Function: pop
Arguments: None
Results: stuff
Errors: None

This function causes the stack to be popped and **stuff** returned.

Function: toptoi
Arguments: None
Results: An actual value in integer form.
Errors: None

The stack is popped. If the popped entry is an **lvalue**, it is converted to an actual. Otherwise, the datum in **stuff** is used. If the resulting datum is of size 2 or of class greater than 0 (i.e., a two-byte address) it is returned. If the datum is of size 1 and class 0, it is first converted to an equivalent two-byte integer and then returned.

Function: eq
Arguments: None
Results: None
Errors: Left-value error

The top level is popped and converted to an actual if necessary. The next level is popped and must be an **lvalue** or an **lvalue** error is raised. The value referenced by the **lvalue** is replaced by the actual. Eight bits are replaced if the **lvalue** represents a **class** 0 eight-bit datum (i.e., a character). Sixteen bits are replaced if the **lvalue** represents a **class** greater than 0 (i.e., an address) or a 16-bit datum of **class** 0 (i.e., an integer).

STATEMENT SCANNING AND ANALYZING

The scanning tools are functions used by the tiny-c Interpreter to recognize tokens of the language. They do not themselves prescribe the language; in fact, they could be used in parsers of languages other than tiny-c. The analyzing tools impart semantics or meaning to the tokens produced by the scanning tools. These are the functions that are the keepers of the definition of tiny-c.

Most of these tools make use of the contents of the global variable **cursor**. This is the address of the next character to be examined in the tiny-c program being interpreted. We say that the "cursor points to" that character. Some of these tools "advance the cursor," i.e., increment the address in **cursor** so that it points to a character further on in the program.

The scanning functions are:

lit
skip
symname

const
rem
blanks

Together they comprise the source code file SCAN.C.

Function: lit
Arguments: The address of the first byte of a character string which is to be matched. The string is terminated by a null byte.
Results: A flag signalling match or no match.
Errors: None

The cursor is first advanced over blanks. If the next characters match the literal, then the cursor is advanced beyond them and a match is signalled. Otherwise, the cursor remains on the first non-blank character and no match is signalled.

Function: skip
Arguments: A left delimiter and a right delimiter, each a single character.
Results: None
Errors: Cursor runaway

The cursor is advanced beyond a balanced pair of left and right delimiters. It is assumed that one left delimiter has already been matched. Cursor runaway occurs when a character beyond progend is being examined.

Function: symname
Arguments: None
Results: A flag signalling match or no match.
Errors: None

The cursor is first advanced over blanks. Then, if the next set of characters is a symbol, the cursor is advanced beyond it, the global variable fname is pointed at its first character, the global variable lname to its last, and a match is signalled. Otherwise, the cursor remains on the first non-blank character and a no match is signalled. A symbol is an alphabetic character followed by an arbitrary number of alphanumeric characters or underscore.

Function: const
Arguments: None
Results: A flag signalling match or no match and the type of constant matched.
Errors: Cursor runaway

The **cursor** is first advanced over blanks. Then one of three types of constants is matched:

1) Number: An optional plus or minus followed by any number of digits.
2) Quoted String: "Anything" which is surrounded by matched double quotes, or which begins with a double quote and is followed by a null byte.
3) Primed String: Anything surrounded by matched single quotes.

If a number is matched, **fname** and **lname** are pointed to its first and last significant characters, including the sign if present. The cursor is advanced beyond the last digit.

If a quoted string is matched, **fname** is pointed at the first byte after the first quote; **lname** is not used. The second quote is replaced by a null byte, and the cursor is advanced beyond this null. This makes string constants conform to the tiny-c convention that character strings end with a null.

If a primed string is matched, **fname** points to the first byte after the first prime. **lname** is not used. The second prime is not modified, and **cursor** is advanced beyond the second prime.

Function:	rem
Arguments:	None
Results:	None
Errors:	Cursor runaway

This function advances **cursor** past all remarks, carriage returns, tabs, and blanks.

Function:	blanks
Arguments:	None
Results:	None
Errors:	None

The **blanks** function advances **cursor** beyond blanks, tabs, and carriage returns.

The tiny-c *statement analyzer* is a collection of eleven subroutines which analyze and evaluate tiny-c statements. These routines are contained in two source code files. ANALYZE.C contains

asgn
expr
factor
reln
skipst
st
term
valloc

and ENTER.C contains

enter
link
setarg

The eight functions in ANALYZE.C are documented in this section. The three functions in ENTER.C are documented in the next section on linking, calling and invoking.

Figure 4-4 figure shows the calling relationship among the 11 routines, the action of which is described briefly below.

link	Builds the first two variable table layers.
st	Determines the kind of statement currently being analyzed and keeps track of the level of statement compounding.
skipst	Moves **cursor** beyond a complete, possibly compound, statement without interpreting it.
valloc	Recognizes variables in **int** and **char** statements, and calls **newvar** to allocate them.
asgn	Matches expressions and calls **eq** to perform any assignments.
reln	Evaluates an expression by calling **expr**. If a relational operator follows the expression, evaluates the next expression and then evaluates the relation between the two expressions.
expr	Evaluates unary plus and minus of a term and binary plus and minus between terms. Calls **term** to evaluate terms.
term	Evaluates multiplication, division, and remainder operators between factors. Calls **factor** to evaluate factors.
factor	Evaluates a factor which is an expression enclosed in parentheses, a constant, or a variable name including a function call. Evaluates function names by calling **enter**.
enter	Transfers control to a function by stacking the current position of **cursor** and setting **cursor** to the beginning of the function. Allocates a new layer in the function table by calling **newfun** and assigns argument values to local variables by calling **setarg**.
setarg	Assigns function argument values in a function call to the local variables used in the definition of the function. Enters local variable names in the variable table by calling **nvalloc**.

Another view of the action of each statement analyzer routine is provided by examining the characters and character strings that each routine recognizes and past which it moves **cursor**. Significant cursor movement routines, i.e., routines which move **cursor** beyond things other than blanks and remarks, are **lit**, **const**, **skipst**, and **symname**. Of these, only **lit** can move **cursor** beyond different strings of symbols, depending on its argument. Table 4-1 displays the characters with which each statement analyzer routine calls **lit**; if any of these routines calls **const**, **skipst**, or **symname**, we indicate this fact by enclosing the routine name in angle brackets,< >.

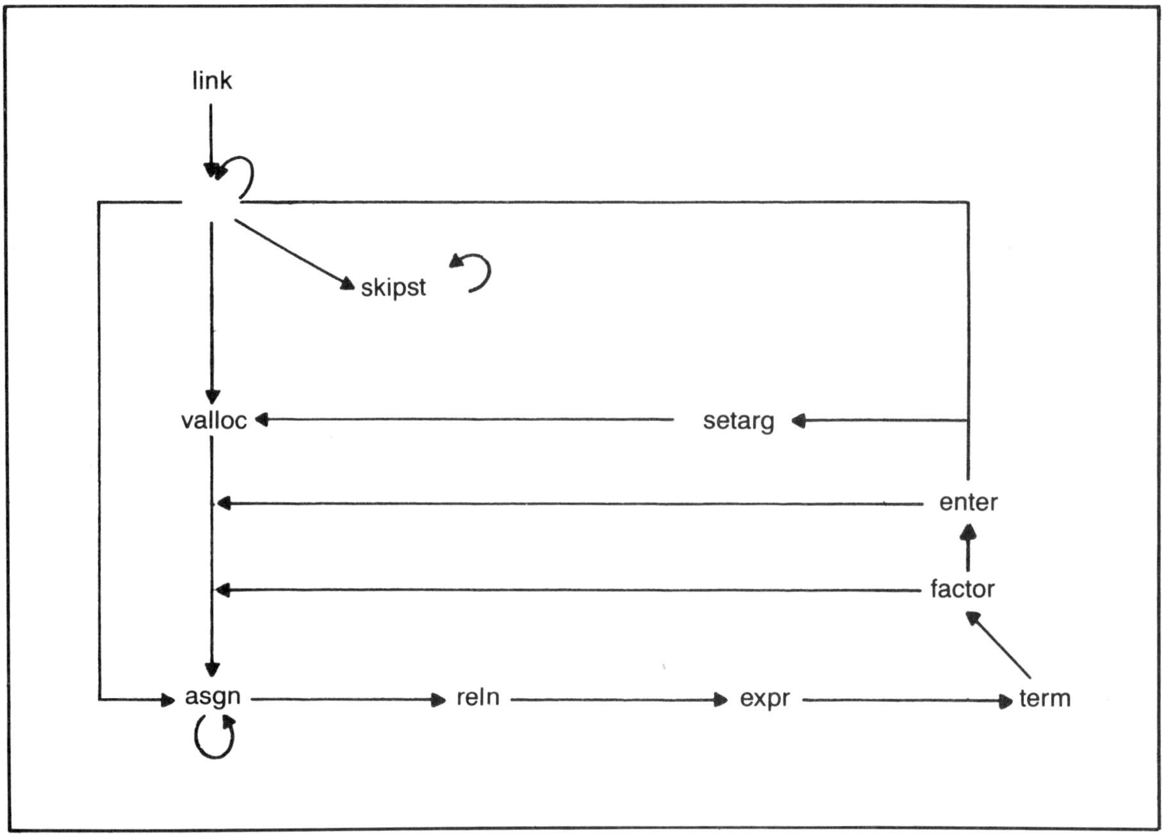

Fig. 4-4. Calling relationship among the eleven subroutines that make up the tiny-c statement analyzer.

Table 4-1. Responses of Statement Analyzer Routines.

st	int char if else while return
enter	int char ( ) , ;
valloc	( )
asgn	=
reln	<= >= == != > <
expr	+ −
term	* / %
factor	( ) MC <const> <symname>
skipst	if else while [(;

The statement analyzer routines communicate with each other by using the tiny-c stack almost exclusively. What is done with the contents of the stack is determined by the position of the cursor and, in the case of **factor** and **valloc**, the setting of the global variables **fname** and **lname**. In the following descriptions, the term *matches* means the routine "recognizes and advances the cursor over the text of," while the term *evaluates* means the routine actually "computes the value of."

Function:	st
Arguments:	None
Results:	None
Errors:	Program segment encountered which is not a tiny-c statement.

This function matches a tiny-c statement; it calls **valloc** to enter global variables in variable table, **asgn** to evaluate relational expressions and **st** to evaluate components of compound statements. Uses **skipst** to skip statements which do not need to be evaluated.

Function:	valloc
Arguments:	A class value and a value of that class.
Results:	Address of first byte of allocated space.
Errors:	Invalid symbol name or invalid array size defining expression.

The **valloc** function matches a variable declaration and enters its name and attributes in the variable table by calling **newvar**. The initial value of the variable name is the passed value of that class. In the case of arrays, it evaluates the expression defining the size of the array.

Function:	asgn
Arguments:	None
Results:	Success flag
Errors:	None

The **asgn** function matches an expression. In the case of an assignment operator, it calls **eq** to make the assignment.

Function:	reln
Arguments:	None
Results:	None
Errors:	None

The **reln** function matches an expression and, if it is followed by a relational operator, matches another expression and evaluates the relational operator.

Function: expr
Arguments: None
Results: None
Errors: None

This function matches an optional unary plus or minus followed by one or more terms separated by binary pluses or minuses. If any operators are matched, the expression is evaluated.

Function: term
Arguments: None
Results: None
Errors: None

Function term matches one or more factors separated by multiplication, division, or remainder operators. If any operators are matched, the term is evaluated.

Function: factor
Arguments: None
Results: None
Errors: Expressions without balanced parentheses; class 0 variables with subscripts; undeclared variable names, or unrecognized statement syntaxes.

The factor function matches constants, variable names (including function calls), and expressions enclosed in parentheses. It evaluates constants and variables, and uses enter to evaluate function calls.

Function: skipst
Arguments: None
Results: None
Errors: Cursor runaway

Function skipst advances cursor to the end of a tiny-c statement, beyond any remarks which appear at the end of the statement. Leading remarks are skipped also.

CALLING, LINKING, AND INVOKING

You are by now quite familiar with the concept of one tiny-c function calling another. When this happens, you know that you leave behind the symbols local to the calling function and you activate the symbols local to the called function. Furthermore, the values of the called function's argument variables are set to the values associated with them by the function's call. This is all taken care of by enter and setarg.

Function: enter
Arguments: An address
Results: None
Errors: Number of arguments in function call not equal to number of arguments in function definition.

Function **enter** saves **cursor**, allocates a layer in the function table by calling **newfun**, calls **setarg** to assign function argument values to function local variables, sets cursor to the passed address, matches parameter declarations and assigns them space and values using **setarg**, pops all arguments off the stack, and calls **st**. (Whew!) Upon return from **st**, it restores **cursor**, and deallocates the layer from function table by calling fundone.

Function: setarg
Arguments: The address of an entry in the tiny-c stack and a class value.
Results: None
Errors: None

This function converts the tiny-c stack entry to an actual; then it calls **valloc**, using this value and the passed class value to enter an argument in the variable table as a local variable, the initial value of which is equal to the value passed in the tiny-c stack.

Not surprisingly, the same sort of thing happens when one tiny-c program—such as the Shell—*invokes* another tiny-c program—such as a program you have entered. When you enter the invoked program, you leave behind all the symbols that were global symbols in that program and you activate a new set of global symbols, i.e., the global symbols in the invoked program. This process is taken care of by the link function.

Function: link
Arguments: None
Results: None
Errors: Unidentifiable global declaration or function name not succeeded by a left bracket.

The link function allocates a new layer of the variable table. It enters global variable names, including all function names, in the variable table. If an **endlibrary** statement is encountered, a second new layer is allocated and the entering of global variable names continues.

Each time one program invokes another, we increase the current *application level*.

The tiny-c program loaded by the initial program load function **ipl** is, by definition, the *level zero program*. Usually this is the tiny-c Shell, but it could be any system-type program. When a program uses MC 11 to invoke (not call) another program, the invoked program is given a level one higher than the invoking program. Thus, when the Shell invokes an application—your program, for example—that application runs at level one. An application is also allowed to use MC 11, creating levels higher than one.

Function:	MC 11
Arguments:	Four pointers: **facts**, **start**, **first**, and **last**
Results:	None
Errors:	None

When **MC 11** is called, a tiny-c program is invoked. The text of the program is from **first** to **last**, inclusively. Pointer **last** should point to a statement terminator, while **start** points to a character string which is a tiny-c statement. The statement can be within the invoked program text, i.e. between **first** and **last**—but it need not be. Pointer **facts** points to a four-byte data area where facts about the exit condition of the invoked program are eturned. The error code raised by the the invoked program, if any, is stored in the first two bytes; the value of **cursor** when the program terminated is stored in the second two bytes.

The program text is linked. This causes a new set of global symbols to be defined. Then the first set of local symbols is allocated and the application level is incremented by one. If no error conditions have been raised by these actions, the statement at **start** is executed. Typically this statement is a function call to a function in the program text.

Values generated in running the invoked program are allocated starting at **last + 1**. The invoked program text therefore should be at the beginning of an array that has enough unused space at the end to hold the maximum number of values which could be simultaneously in use by the program.

It is important to notice that the set of system library symbols never changes once it is established by the initial program load. The same set of system library facilities is accessed by all functions and by all program invocations. Even if an invoked program contains an **endlibary** statement, since the **link** function starts a new global symbol set when it finds this statement, the symbols before the **endlibrary** will be ignored at any application level above zero. This means that when necessary information can be transferred between program invocations via system library variables.

An example of the use of application program level is in the **stbegin** routine. We wished to provide a facility for interrupting a runaway application program without creating the possibility of an accidental exit from the Shell. If the application level is greater than zero and there is an ESC character waiting in the keyboard entry buffer before each statement is interpreted, then interpretation is stopped and the program invocation is terminated with the KILL error code.

Another example of using application levels is in using the Shell to program and test new or modified Shells. A working Shell is loaded and started at level zero. An experimental Shell is loaded as a level-one application. It is edited, started, and tested just like any other application. When the level one experimental Shell is running, it is preparing the text of still another program, which, if started, runs at level two.

One thing to pay careful attention to when you're doing this sort of thing is the sizes of program text arrays. Keep in mind that the program text and generated values of each new application program must fit completely within the program text buffer provided by the application program which invokes it.

For example, the program text space allocated in the standard Shell is 12,000 bytes. If you tried to load the standard Shell unchanged into itself, the text of the Shell would occupy roughly the first 5600 bytes of this array. When this text was linked, another 12,000-byte program text array would be cleared at the end of this 5600 bytes. Since the original array was only 12,000 bytes long, you would be clearing memory locations outside the original array and in the value space of the invoking Shell. Obviously, the results would be disastrous. When you developing one Shell inside another, be sure that the program space in the new Shell is much smaller than the one in the Shell you are using to build it.

MAIN, CUSTOMIZATION, AND UTILITY ROUTINES

The main routine for the tiny-c Interpreter is in the source code file MAIN.C, all by itself.

Function:	main
Arguments:	An optional file name
Results:	None
Errors:	Unable to open the argument file if given

The main routine initializes the 18 global variables and then calls ipl to load the program buffer with TINYC.IPL if no file name has been specified; otherwise, it loads the buffer with the contents of the file named in the argument. If the call to ipl is successful, main calls link to build the first two layers of the variable table. If link is successful, main calls newfun to allocate the first local variable layer and then calls st with cursor pointing to the beginning of the program buffer.

Customization Routines

Customization routines are user-supplied routines that are called at specific points in the processing cycle of the tiny-c interpreter. They give the user the opportunity to interrogate the current state of the interpreter, perhaps changing either the data or the program flow based on these investigations. The five customization routines are:

ipl
stbegin
prbegin
prdone
usermc

and they are located in the source code file CUSTOM.C.

Function: ipl
Arguments: A file name
Results: None
Errors: Unable to open the argument file

The ipl routine is called by the tiny-c main program to load the program in the argument file into the internal program buffer. Since the material in the named file may not have been written out by tiny-c (but may have been prepared, in fact, by using a non-tiny-c editor, the ipl function must translate between the file format used by the program that made the file and the program text format expected by tiny-c. Namely, lines are terminated by a single new-line character (ASCII LF or 10_{10}) and there are no null characters (ASCII NUL or 0_{10}).

Function: stbegin
Arguments: None
Results: None
Errors: None

The stbegin routine is called by the tiny-c Interpreter just before it begins to interpret each statement. It provides the user with the opportunity to monitor the progress of program execution, or to interrupt interpretation by raising an error condition. The off-the-shelf version of stbegin checks for an ESC character waiting as keyboard input. If an ESC character is waiting and the application level of the program being interpreted is greater than zero, then the KILL error flag is raised and the ESC character is cleared from the input queue. The effect is to provide a way to interrupt runaway application programs by pressing the Escape key.

Function: prbegin
Arguments: None
Results: None
Errors: None

The tiny-c Interpreter calls the prbegin routine just before it starts an application program. In the off-the-shelf version of tiny-c, prbegin is a null function.

Function: prdone
Arguments: None
Results: None
Errors: None

The tiny-c Interpreter calls the prdone routine just after it exits from an application program. In the off-the-shelf version of tiny-c, prdone is a null function.

One example of a possibility for the use of the prbegin, stbegin, and prdone customization functions is adding an interactive debugging capability to tiny-c. Function **prbegin** could set up data structures which would be used to track the execution of a program, **stbegin** could update these structures and show the user what was happening, and **prdone** could prepare the structures for analysis after the program being debugged exists.

Function:	usermc
Arguments:	Number of arguments and user MC number
Results:	None
Errors:	Invalid MC number or incorrect number of arguments

The **mc** routine calls **usermc** whenever the MC number given in an MC call is greater than 999. The MC number passed to **usermc** is 1000 less than the number given in the MC call. For details on MC calls, see the last section in this chapter. The off-the-shelf version of **usermc** implements three MC routines to access the sound system on the PCjr.

Utility Routines

The utility routines supply general-purpose services to the rest of the interpreter including the MC handling routines. The four utility routines are

error
mcerror
movn
wait

and are in the source code file UTILITY.C.

Function:	error
Arguments:	Error number
Results:	None
Errors:	None

If there is no outstanding error, **error** sets the **err** global variable to the argument and the **errat** global variable to the current value of **cursor**.

Function:	mcerror
Arguments:	Number of arguments to **MC** besides the MC number
Results:	None
Errors:	None

The **mcerror** function pops argument number of values off the tiny-c stack and calls **error** with MCERR.

Function: movn

Arguments:	To address, from address, number of bytes
Results:	None
Errors:	None

Function movn moves number of bytes from the "from" address to the "to" address without regard for overlap.

Function:	wait
Arguments:	Number of ticks
Results:	None
Errors:	None

Function wait uses the PC system clock to wait ticks tenths of a second.

MACHINE CALL ROUTINES

Machine call routines are used for two primary reasons. The first reason is to connect tiny-c programs to the computing environment in which they are being run. On the IBM PC and PCjr this environment consists of the services of the disk operating system and the facilities of the 8088 processor and its support chips. The second reason is to increase the runtime speed of a tiny-c program by implementing oft-used functions in machine code, rather than in interpreted tiny-c code.

If you write a machine language subroutine which you want to call from a tiny-c program, the mechanism for doing so is the machine-call MC function. MC receives passed arguments and returns a value, just like any other tiny-c function. An argument can be an arbitrary expression. For example, you can write:

```
k = MC(row-1, 2*col+6, 1, 1001)
```

This passes four arguments to MC; the returned value is assigned to k.

MC can be used in an if statement, or an expression, or anywhere else a function can be used:

```
if (MC(12)= ='x') gotcha(MC(2))
```

This calls MC with the argument 12. If it returns the value x, then MC is called again with the argument 2. The result returned is used as the argument in a call to gotcha.

The MC function (the sole occupant of source code file MC.C) differs from other tiny-c functions in three ways:

1) Its name, MC, is built into tiny-c.
2) It can have a variable number of arguments, but must have at least one. (Other functions must have exactly the number of arguments—including none—specified in their definitions.)
3) It is coded in machine language, not in tiny-c.

The last argument determines which particular machine-coded function is to be executed. This argument is called the MC *function number*.

Every **MC** function is assigned a unique number. Those furnished as system machine calls have numbers from 1 to 999. Those you write for your own local use can be assigned numbers from 1000 to 32767. This number assignment system guarantees that a future release of tiny-c won't have new function numbers that conflict with your own local functions.

The tiny-c Interpreter evaluates the arguments to an **MC** call and pushes their values on the tiny-c stack. It then calls the **MC** function with the number of arguments that it found.

Function:	**MC**
Arguments:	Number of arguments in call.
Results:	None
Errors:	None

The last argument is the MC function number. It is popped from the tiny-c stack and examined. If it is less than 1000, the appropriate system MC is executed. If the MC function number exceeds 999, then 1000 is subtracted from it and a subroutine call is made to **usermc**.

All **MC** code is obligated to pop all arguments besides the **MC** function number off the tiny-c stack and push a value for the **MC** call onto the stack. The routine **toptoi** may be used to get values off the stack; the routines **push** and **pushint** may be used to push the result value onto the stack. Remember that the argument values are pushed onto the stack left-to-right so **toptoi** will return them right-to-left!

If the wrong number of arguments are on the stack, the routine **mcerror** may be called to clear the arguments off the stack, raise the **MCERR** flag, and push a zero result value onto the stack.

The **MC** and **usermc** routines supplied with the tiny-c package are both written in C and use the DeSmet C runtime package to interface to DOS and the IBM PC hardware. If you are not going to use this C compiler to rebuild tiny-c, then you will have to translate these routines into the machine language facility you plan to use. This could be another C compiler, a compiler for another language, or an assembler.

SLOAN

Appendices

Appendix A

tiny-c Shell Commands

Command	Name	Arguments	Description
c	change	/string-1/string-2/	**Action:** Replace string-1 with string-2 in the current line; the slash (/) can be any character not appearing string-1 or string-2. **Default:** If no arguments are given, the previous change command is repeated.
d	delete	n	**Action:** Delete n lines, starting at the current line. **Default:** If not given, n is taken to be 1.
l	locate	/string/	**Action:** The program text is searched forward starting at the current line for the first appearance of string; the slash (/) may be any character

Command	Name	Arguments	Description
			not appearing in string. **Default:** If no argument is given, the previous locate command is repeated.
p	print	n	**Action: Print** n lines starting with the current line. **Default:** If not given, n is taken to be 1.
r	read	filename	**Action:** The contents of the file named **filename** are appended to the end of the program text.
w	write	filename	**Action:** The contents of the program text area are written to the file named **file name**.
x	exit	(none)	**Action:** tiny-c exits and returns to DOS.
+	next	n	**Action:** The current line number isincremented by n. **Default:** If not given, n is taken to be 1.
–	last	n	**Action:** The current line number is decremented by n. **Default:** If not given, n is taken to be 1.

Command	Name	Arguments	Description
/	status	(none)	**Action:** Prints the current line number, the total number of lines, the total number of characters used, and the total number of characters unused.

Appendix B

tiny-c Error Codes

1 Illegal statement
2 Cursor ran off end of program. Look for missing] or).
3 Symbol error. A name was expected. For example, 10 + + will cause this.
5 Right parenthesis missing, as in x = (x + b*b.
6 Subscript out of range.
7 Using a pointer as a variable or vice versa.
9 More expression expected, as in x = x +.
14 Illegal equal sign, as in 7=2
16 Stack overflow. Either an expression is too tough or you are too deeply nested in functions or a recursion has gone too deep.
17 Too many active functions.
18 Too many active variables.
19 Too many active values. Values share space with program text. Squeeze the program and this error may go away.
20 Startup error. Caused by a "garbage" line outside of all brackets [ ], i.e., where globals are declared. A missing [or] can cause this.
21 Arguments needed and number given don't agree.
22 A function body must begin with [.
24 An illegal invocation of MC.
26 Undefined symbol. Perhaps a variable name is misspelled, or you need an int or char statement for it, or a function isn't loaded.
99 Program interrupted.

Appendix C

The tiny-c System Library

The system library includes functions that do input, output, and character manipulation. The definitions given here show the declaration of the function name and the arguments, if any.

gs char buffer(0)

Reads a line, i.e., a string of characters terminated by a carriage return, from the terminal and puts it in **buffer**. The carriage return at the end of the line is changed to a null byte. The value of the function is the number of characters placed in **buffer** excluding the null byte. A value of 0 is permitted.

ps char buffer (0)

Prints the string in **buffer** on the screen. A null byte signals the end of the string. The null is not transmitted. The number of characters transmitted is returned as the value of the function.

pl char buffer(0)

The same as **ps** but prints the string on a new line. The number of characters transmitted, not including the leading return and line feed, is returned.

pn int n

Prints the value of **n** on the screen preceded by a blank.

The number of characters transmitted, including the blank, is returned.

gn

Reads a line and returns the integer at the beginning of the line. If there is no integer there, it prints "number required" and tries again.

gc

Reads a line and returns the first character on the line.

putchar char c

Transmits the character **c** to the terminal. Any character, including control characters, can be transmitted, except that a quote is transmitted if **c** is null. The character **c** is returned.

getchar

Reads and returns a character from the terminal. Any character, including control characters, can be read by this function.

readfile char name (0), where (0), limit (0)
int unit

Reads data from a file. The **name** argument is a character string terminated by a null byte; **where** and **limit** are pointers. The **unit** designator is an input/output unit number. The file with name **name** is opened for reading on device **unit**. All of its records are read and placed in sequentially higher addresses, starting at **where** but in no case going beyond **limit**. Then **unit** is closed. If successful, the total number of bytes read is returned. If **limit** is exceeded, the message "too big" is printed and −2 is returned.

writefile char name(0), from(0), to(0)
int unit

Writes data to a file. The **name** argument is a character string terminated by a null byte; **from** and **to** are pointers. The **unit** argument is an input/output unit number. Function **writefile** opens unit **unit** for output. The contents of sequentially higher addresses from **from** to **to** inclusive are written to **unit** as a file named **name**. Then the file is closed. If successful, the total number of bytes written is returned. If a problem occurs, a negative value is returned.

num char b(5)
int v(0)

Converts a string of digits without leading sign or blanks

to the corresponding numeric value, which is put in **v(0)**. The first non-digit stops the conversion. At most, five digits are examined. The number of bytes converted is returned as the value of the function. Note that the second argument must be a pointer to an integer.

atoi char b(0) **int v(0)**	Converts a character string of this form: 0 or more blanks optional + or – character 0 or more blanks 0 to 5 digits to its numeric value, which is put in **v(0)**. The first non-digit following the digit part stops the conversion. The number of characters in **b** that were used to form the value is returned as the value of the function.
ceqn char a(0), b(0) **int n**	Compares two character strings for equality for **n** characters. Returns 1 on equals, 0 on not-equals.
alpha char c	Returns a 1 if **c** is an alphabetic character, upper- or lowercase. Otherwise returns a 0.
index char s1(0) **int n1** **char s2(0)** **int n2**	Finds the leftmost copy of the character string **s1**, which is **n1** bytes long in the character string **s2**, which is **n2** bytes long. If **s1** does not appear in **s2**, 0 is returned. If **s1** does appear, returns **n + 1** such that **s2 + n** points to the first character of the copy in **s2**.
move char a(0), b(0)	Moves string **a** into **b** up to and including the null byte of **a**.
movebl char a(0), b(0) **int k**	Moves a block of storage up or down **k** bytes in memory; **a** and **b** point to the first and last characters of the block to be moved. If **k** is positive, the move is to higher addresses, and if it is negative the move is to lower addresses. If **k** is positive, the byte at **b** is moved first, then the byte at **b – 1**, etc. If **k** is negative, the byte at **a** is moved first. Large blocks thus can be moved a few bytes without destruction.
countch char a(0), **b(0), c**	Counts the instances of the character **c** in the block of storage from **a** to **b** inclusive and returns the count.

scann char from(0),
to (0), c
int n(0)

Scans from **from** to **to** inclusive for instances of the character **c**. The integer **n(0)** is decremented for each **c** found. If **n(0)** reaches 0, or if the character in **to(0)** is examined, **scann** stops. Function **scann** returns the offset relative to the pointer **from** to the last examined character. Thus, if the third character position after **from** is the last examined, **scann** returns 3.

chrdy

Returns a copy of an input character from the terminal if a character has been typed but not yet read by another function, except that if the typed character is a null, a 1 is returned. If no unread character has been typed, a null byte is returned. The character is not cleared so a subsequent call to **getchar** or **gc** will return the same character.

pft char a(0), b(0)

Transfers all characters from **a** to **b** inclusive to the screen.

fopen int rw
char name(0)
int size, unit

Opens or creates a file for access on logical unit number **unit**. The **name** variable contains a null-terminated string giving the name of the file. The file is opened for reading if **rw** is 1, and writing if **rw** is 2. If **rw** is 2 and the file does not exist, then it will be created and its size guaranteed to be at least **size** bytes. Otherwise **size** is ignored, but it must be given. If no error is detected, a 0 is returned. If an error is detected a nonzero value is returned.

fread char a(0)
int unit

Starting at **a**, reads into memory the next 512-byte record of data from the file opened on unit number **unit**. The array **a** must be large enough to hold an entire record. The length in bytes of the record actually placed at **a** is returned as the value of **fread**. A value of −1 is returned if an end-of-file is detected.

fwrite char from(0),
to (0)
int unit

Writes one record with the bytes from **from** to **to** inclusive to the file opened on unit number **unit**. This becomes the next record of the file. Its length is **to-from + 1**; this is the length that will be returned when the record is read by **fread**.

fclose int unit

The file opened on unit number **unit** is made permanent and arrangements are made for end-of-file detection by **fread**.

beep int f, d

The beeper is sounded at frequency **f** for **d** tenths of a second.

Appendix D

System and User Machine Calls for the IBM PC and PCjr

These machine calls are furnished with the tiny-c Interpreter. They are always loaded and available for use, and are called as described in Chapter 4. The function number is the *last* argument. Thus, MC 1 is called like this:

```
MC ('x', 1)
```

Where no results are indicated, a zero is returned as the value of the MC.

Function: MC(character, 1)
Arguments: A character value.
Results: None
Errors: None
Action: character is transmitted to the screen.

Function: MC(2)
Arguments: None
Results: A character value.
Errors: None
Action: A character is retrieved from the console terminal and returned as the value of the function. The input port from the console terminal is cleared to receive another character.

Function: MC(mode, name, size, channel, 3)
Arguments: A mode, file name, file size, and channel number.
Results: An open status indicator.
Errors: None
Action: Same as **fopen** in the standard library (see Appendix C).

Function: MC (buffer, channel, 4)
Arguments: Pointer and a channel number.
Results: A get-status indicator.
Errors: None
Action: Same as **fread** in the standard library (see Appendix C).

Function: MC (from, to, 5)
Arguments: Two pointers and a channel number.
Results: A put-status indicator.
Errors: None
Action: Same as **fwrite** in the standard library (see Appendix C).

Function: MC (channel, 6)
Arguments: A channel number.
Results: None
Errors: None
Action: Same as **fclose** in the standard library (see Appendix C).

Function: MC (from, to, bytes, 7)
Arguments: Two pointers and an integer.
Results: None
Errors: None
Action: Same as **moveb1** in the standard library (see Appendix C).

Function: MC (from, to, character, 8)
Arguments: Two pointers and a character value.
Results: The number of appearances of the character between the two pointers, inclusively.
Errors: None
Action: Same as **countch** in the standard library (see Appendix C).

Function: MC (from, to, character, nptr, 9)
Arguments: Two pointers, a character value, and an integer pointer.
Results: A pointer to the last character examined.
Errors: None
Action: Same as **scann** in the standard library (see Appendix C).

Function:	MC (10)
Arguments:	None
Results:	None
Errors:	None
Action:	An immediate return to the operating system.

Function:	MC (facts, start, first, last, 11)
Arguments:	Four pointers.
Results:	None
Errors:	None
Action:	See Chapter 4.

Function:	MC (12)
Arguments:	None
Results:	A character value.
Errors:	None
Action:	Same as chrdy in the standard library (see Appendix C).

Function:	MC (from, to, 13)
Arguments:	Two pointers.
Results:	None
Errors:	None
Action:	Same as pft in the standard library (see Appendix C).

Function:	MC (n, 14)
Arguments:	An integer.
Results:	None
Errors:	None
Action:	Same as pn in the standard library (see Appendix C).

Function:	MC (buffer, 15)
Arguments:	A character buffer.
Results:	None
Errors:	None
Action:	Same as gs in the standard library (see Appendix C).

Function:	MC (start, bytes, character, 16)
Arguments:	A pointer, a number of bytes, a character.
Results:	None
Errors:	None
Action:	The argument number of bytes starting at start are set to character.

Function: MC (frequency, duration, 17)
Arguments: Two integers.
Results: None
Errors: None
Action: Same as **beep** in the standard library (see Appendix C).

In addition to the seventeen standard machine calls, the IBM PC and PCjr version of tiny-c comes with three user machine calls. They are included primarily to demonstrate the use of user machine calls. They implement an interface to the sound system of the PCjr.

Function: MC (noise_type, attenuation, 1000)
Arguments: Two integers.
Results: **None**
Errors: None
Action: The noise generator is turned on. The **noise_type** is coded as follows:

0 periodic noise shifted at 6992 Hz
1 periodic noise shifted at 3496 Hz
2 periodic noise shifted at 1748 Hz
3 periodic noise shifted by tone voice 2
4 white noise shifted at 6992 Hz
5 white noise shifted at 3496 Hz
6 white noise shifted at 1748 Hz
7 white noise shifted by tone voice 2

and the **attenuation** is coded as follows:

0 OFF
1 28 dB
2 26 dB
3 24 dB
4 22 dB
5 20 dB
6 18 dB
7 16 dB
8 14 dB
9 12 dB
10 10 dB
11 8 dB
12 6 dB
13 4 dB
14 2 dB

Function: MC (voice, frequency, attenuation, 1001)

Arguments: Three integers.
Results: None
Errors: None
Action: Tone generator voice is turned on at the frequency and attenuation. Attenuation is coded as above and voice is 0, 1, or 2.

Function: MC (frequency, 1002)
Arguments: An integer.
Results: None
Errors: None
Action: The frequency of the most recently mentioned tone generator voice is changed to frequency.

Appendix E

The Standard tiny-c IPL File

The standard tiny-c initial program load file TINYC.IPL consists of the system library functions followed by an **endlibrary** statement and then the tiny-c Shell program. The boot program is simply a call to the **main** function of the shell.

Except for slight variations in the code for a few functions, the versions of the IPL and tiny-c Shell files listed in this appendix are identical and fully compatible with those found on the tiny-c disk. To conserve storage space and increase execution speed, the comments included here are omitted in the "lean and mean" disk version, as are the helpful (but ultimately unnecessary) indentations and extra line feeds between brackets. If the identifiers used in these listings seem to you to be running exactly counter to the recommendation (and tiny-c's capacity) for meaningful function and variable names, it is for the same set of reasons. Identifiers for the disk version have been "crunched" from longer, more descriptive names that appear as comments beside the appropriate declaration statements.

```
/* Boot the tiny-c Shell

[main();]

/*===========================================================================*/
/*                 The tiny-c Standard System Library Functions              */
/*===========================================================================*/

/* Transmits c to the terminal.  If c is null transmits ".
```

```
putchar char c
[
   if(c==0)c='"'
   return MC c,1
]

/* Reads one character from the terminal

getchar
[
   return MC 2
]

/* Reads a line from the terminal.  Implements character and line delete.

gs char b(0)
[
   return MC b,15
]

/* Prints everything between two addresses

pft char f(0),t(0)  /* from(0), to(0) */
[
   MC f,t,13
]

/* Prints a string

ps char b(0)
[
   int l
   char c
   l=-1
   while((c=b(l=l+1))!=0)MC c,1
   return l
]

/* Goes to a new line and prints a string

pl char b(0)
[
   MC 13,1;MC 10,1
   ps b
]

/* Tests if a is alphabetic

alpha char a

[
   if((a>='a')*(a<='z'))return 1
   if((a>='A')*(a<='Z'))return 1
]

/* Converts numeric character string b to integer, puts value in b(0)
/* Returns number of bytes examined.  First non-digit stops the scan.

num char b(5)
    int v(0)
```

```
[
   int k
   v(0)=0
   while(k<5) [
      if((b(k)<'0')+(b(k)>'9'))return k
      v(0)=10*v(0)+b(k)-'0'
      k=k+1
   ]
   return k
]

/* Converts signed integer character string b to binary integer, and
/* puts value in v(0).  Returns number of bytes examined.

atoi char b(0)
     int v(0)
[
   int k,s
   char c
   s=1
   c=b(0)
   while((c==' ')+(c=='-')+(c=='+')) [
      if(c=='-')s=-1
      c=b(k=k+1)
   ]
   k=k+num(b+k,v)
   v(0)=s*v(0)
   return k
]

/* Prints a signed integer

pn int n
[
   MC ' ',1
   MC n,14
]

/* Reads a line from the terminal, gets a signed integer from the
/* beginning of the line and returns its value.
/* Insists on getting a number

gn
[
   char b(20)
   int v(0)
   while(1) [
      gs b
      if(atoi b,v)return v(0)
      ps"number required "
   ]
]

/* Compares first n bytes starting at a, with first n starting at b.
/* Returns 1 on match or 0 on no match.

ceqn char a(0),b(0)
     int n
[
   int k
```

```
   k=-1
   while((k=k+1)<n)if(a(k)!=b(k))return 0
   return 1
]

/* Searches string i of length l for the first occurrence of the
/* string f (of length n).  Returns 0 on not found or n>0 on found,
/* where n is the offset from i-1 where f was found.
index char i(0)      /* in(0)   */
      int l          /* lin     */
      char f(0)      /* find(0) */
      int n          /* lfind   */
[
   if(n<=0)return 1                         /* Null text always found
   if(l<=0)return 0
   int a,d(0)        /* at, left(0) */
   while(a+n<=l) [
      d(0)=1
      a=a+1+scann(i+a,i+l-n,f(0),d)         /* scann finds first char fast
      if(d(0))return 0                      /* If no first char then fail
      if(ceqn(i+a,f+1,n-1))return a         /* If match, then succeed
   ]
]

/* Move string a to b.  First null in a stops the move.

move char a(0),b(0)
[
   int k
   int l(0)
   l(0)=1
   k=scann(a,a+32765,0,l)
   movebl(a,a+k,b-a)                        /* Move null too
   return k                                 /* Number of bytes moved
]


/* Read a line, return its first character.

gc
[
   char f
   f=MC 2
   while(MC(2)!=10) []
   return f
]

/* Move the block a...b up or down n bytes.

movebl char a(0),b(0);int n
[
   MC a,b,n,7
]

/* In the block a...b count the occurrences of character c.

countch char a(0),b(0),c
[
   return MC a,b,c,8
]
```

```
/* Scan the block from a to b for the n(0)th occurrence of
/* character c.  Reduce n(0) for every c found.  Return pointer
/* to last character examined.

scann char a(0),b(0),c;int n(0)
[
   return MC a,b,c,n,9
]

/* Test for a character waiting from the terminal.

chrdy
[
   return MC 12
]

/* Read the filename into w, but take care not to read into bytes
/* beyond limit.  Use u to do the read.

readfile char n(0),w(0),l(0)  /* name(0), where(0), limit(0) */
         int u                /* unit                         */
[
   int k,t                    /* k, total */
   if(MC(1,n,0,u,3)<0) [      /* Open  */
      pl"File not found"
      MC(u,6)                 /* Close */
      return -1
   ]
   while(w+511<=l) [
      k=MC(w,u,4)                       /* Read a block
      if(k== -1) [MC(u,6);return t;]    /* End of file
      if(k<  -1) [MC(u,6);return k;]    /* Error
      w=w+k
      t=t+k
   ]
   pl"Too big"
   MC(u,6)
   return -2
]

/* Write the file from b to e as a file named n, using u
/* to do the writing.

writefile char n(0),b(0),e(0)           /* name(0), from(0), to(0) */
          int u                         /* unit                    */
[
   int k,t,l                            /* k, total, l */
   if(MC(2,n,e-b+1,u,3)<0) [            /* Open for writing
      pl"Unit 1 open"
      MC(u,6)
      return -1
   ]
   while(b<=e) [
      l=e-b
      if(l>511)l=511                    /* Blocksize-1 for the installation
      k=MC(b,b+l,u,5)                   /* Write one block
      if(k<0) [MC(u,6);return k;]       /* Error
      t=t+l+1
      b=b+l+1
   ]
```

```
   MC(u,6)                                     /* Write end-of-file
   return t                                    /* No error, return amount written
]

/* Open a file
fopen int rw                /* mode       */
      char n(0)             /* name(0)    */
      int s,u               /* size, unit */
[
   return MC(rw,n,s,u,3)
]

/* Read a record from a file

fread char a(0)
      int u               /* unit */
[
   return MC(a,u,4)
]

/* Write a record to a file

fwrite char f(0),t(0)     /* from(0), to(0) */
       int u              /* unit           */
[
   return MC(f,t,u,5)
]

/* Close a file

fclose int u              /* unit */
[
   return MC(u,6)
]


beep int f,d              /* frequency, duration */
[
   MC f,d,17
]

endlibrary


/*==========================================================================*/
/*                        The Standard tiny-c Shell                          */
/*==========================================================================*/

int er(0)        /* err      */    Error returned by application program
int cu           /* cursor   */    Pointer into current line
int lo           /* lineno   */    Current line number
int pe           /* progend  */    Pointer to last byte of program
int lp           /* lpr      */    Length of pr
int ll           /* lline    */    Length of input line
int la           /* lastline */    Number of lines in pr
int fl           /* len      */    Length of ft
int tl           /* tolen    */    Length of tt
char ft(40)      /* ltext    */    Locate text
char tt(80)      /* totext   */    Change-to text
char ln(133)     /* line     */    Input line
```

```
char pr(12000)    /* pr        */    Program buffer

main

[
   char c
   int v(1)    /* val(1) */
   lp=12000
   pr(0)=10                              /* Create empty line 0
   while(1) [

   ps"tc>"
      while((ll=gs(ln))==0) []           /* Read non-empty line
      c=ln(0)
      if(c=='.') [                       /* If dot, do it now
         if(num(ln+1,v))go(v)            /* .number
         else if((ln(2)==0)+(alpha(ln(2))==0)) [
            c=ln(1)                      /* One-letter commands */
               if(c=='p')pt              /* print               */
               else if(c=='d')dl         /* dlines              */
               else if(c=='l')oi         /* locline             */
               else if(c=='c')ch         /* change              */
               else if(c=='/')fa         /* facts               */
               else if(c=='r')gi         /* progin              */
               else if(c=='w')gu         /* progout             */
               else if(c=='x')return
               else [ps"???";pl""]
         ]else st                        /* If multi-letter command then start
      ]                                  /* If not a dot, try + and -
      else if(c=='-')up                  /* up                  */
      else if(c=='+')do                  /* down                */
      else in                            /* insert              */
   ]
]

/* Prints n lines, making the last current

pi int n                /* plines, n      */
[
   int f,l,v(0)         /* fc, lc, val(0) */
   v(0)=n
   f=fc                                  /* First character to print
   lo=lo+v(0)-1
   l=cu+scann(pr+cu,pr+pe,10,v)          /* Last character to print
   cu=l
   lo=lo-v(0)
   MC pr+f,pr+l,13                       /* This does the printing
]

/* Returns pointer to first character of current line

fc                      /* fchar */
[
   int k
   if((k=cu)==0)return 0
   while(pr(k=k-1)!=10)if(k<=0)break
   return k+1
]

/* Returns pointer to last character of current line
```

```
lc                        /* lchar */
[
   int k
   k=cu-1
   while(pr(k=k+1)!=10)if(k>=pe)break
   return k
]

/* Advances cursor (cu) to next line

nl
[
   if((cu=lc()+1)>pe) [
      cu=pe
      return 0
   ]
   return lo=lo+1
]

/* Backs cursor to previous line

bl
[
   if((cu=fc()-1)<0)cu=0
   else lo=lo-1
]

/* Prints a set of lines

pt                        /* print  */
[
   int v(0)               /* val(0) */
   if(ln(2))num(ln+3,v)
   else v(0)=1
   pi(v(0))
]

/* Deletes a set of lines

dl                        /* dlines */
[
   int f,l,v(1)           /* fc, lc, val(1) */
   if(cu==0) [
      ps"cannot delete line 0";pl""
      return
   ]
   if(ln(2)==0)v(0)=1
   else num(ln+3,v)                       /* v is how many lines to delete
   la=la-v(0)
   f=fc                                   /* First char to delete
   l=cu+scann(pr+cu,pr+pe,10,v)           /* Last char to delete
   la=la+v(0)                             /* If v is too big, adjust
                                          /* la by the excess
   lo=lo-1                                /* Back up the current line
   cu=f-1
   if(l<pe)movebl(pr+l+1,pr+pe,-(l-f+1))/* Close up the non-deleted text
   pe=pe-(l-f+1)
]
```

```
/* Locates a line with given text

oi                      /* locline */
[
   int k
   if(ln(3)==0)return
   if(ln(2)!=0) [
      fl=move(ln+3,ft)                       /* Set up locate text
      if(ft(0)=='^')ft(0)=10
      if(ft(fl-1)=='^')ft(fl-1)=10
   ]
   if(fl==0) [
      pl"locate what?";pl""
      return
   ]                                            /* Scan starts at next line
   if(nl()!=0)[
      if(k=index(pr+cu-1,pe-cu+2,ft,fl)) [    /* Index does the search
         cu=cu-2+k                              /* Found, set cursor
                                                /* and line number
         if(pr(cu)==10)cu=cu+1
         lo=countch(pr,pr+cu-1,10)
         pi 1                                   /* Print found line
      ]
      else[ps"?";pl""]                          /* Not found
   ]
   else[ps"at bottom";pl""]                     /* No next line, cannot start
]

/* Changes text within current line

ch                      /* change      */
[
   char d               /* del         */
   int p,f,l            /* ptr, fc, lc */
   if(ln(2)!=0) [                     /* Default to previous locate, to texts
      d=ln(2)                         /* Delimits locate and to texts
      p=2
      while((ln(p=p+1)!=d) [          /* Find the middle delimiter
         if(ln(p)==0) [               /* No middle delimiter
            ln(p+1)=0                 /* Second null creates empty to text
            break
         ]
      ]
      ln(p)=0                         /* Null in middle delimiter
      fl=move(ln+3,ft)                /* New locate text
      tl=move(ln+p+1,tt)              /* New to text
      if(tl)if(tt(tl-1)==d)tl=tl-1    /* Remove optional third delimiter
   ]
   f=fc                               /* Scan line for ltext
   l=lc()-1
   int k
   if(k=index(pr+f,l-f+1,ft,fl)) [
      cu=f+k-1                        /* Found, set cursor to where
      movebl(pr+cu+fl,pr+pe,tl-fl)    /* move tail-end text in or out
      pe=pe+tl-fl
      if(tl)movebl(tt,tt+tl-1,pr+cu-tt)
   ]
   pi 1
]
```

```
/* Inserts one line of text after current line

in                      /* insert */
[
   ll=ll+1
   if(pe+ll>lp) [
      ps"won't fit";pl""
      return
   ]
   if(nl)movebl(pr+cu,pr+pe,ll)        /* Move tail out
   else[cu=cu+1;lo=lo+1]
   pe=pe+ll
   movebl(ln,ln+ll-1,pr-ln+cu)         /* Move in new line
   pr(cu+ll-1)=10
   la=la+1
]

/* Gives facts about current line, including error code

wh                      /* whathappened */
[
   int f,l,u,b          /* fc, lc, lcurs, blanks */
   pn lo;ps" --- err ";pn er(0);pl""
   u=cu
   f=fc
   b=u-f
   l=lc
   f=f-1
   while((f=f+1)<l)putchar(pr(f));pl""
   while((b=b-1)>=0)putchar(' ')
   putchar '<';pl""
]

/* Move cursor down

do                      /* down   */
[
   int v(1)             /* val(1) */
   if(ln(1)==0)v(0)=1
   else num(ln+1,v)
   lo=lo+v(0)
   v(0)=v(0)+1
   cu=cu+scann(pr+cu,pr+pe,10,v)
   lo=lo-v(0)
   pi(1)
]


up
[
   int v(1)             /* val(1) */
   if(ln(1)==0)v(0)=1
   else num(ln+1,v)
   if((v(0)=lo-v(0))<0) v(0)=0
   go(v)
]

/* Move cursor to given line
```

```
go                          /* goto */
   int l(1)
[
   lo=l(0)
   l(0)=l(0)+1
   cu=scann(pr,pr+pe,10,l)
   lo=lo-l(0)
   pi(1)
]

/* Print some facts

fa                          /* facts */
[
   pn lo;pn la;pn pe;pn lp-pe;pl""
]

/* Invoke an application program

st                          /* start */
[
   MC(ln+ll, 134-ll, ' ', 16)
   MC(er,ln+1,pr+pe,pr,11)
   if(cu<0)cu=0;if(cu>pe)cu=pe
   lo=countch(pr,pr+cu-1,10)
   pl"";
   if(er(0))
      if(er(0)==99)[ps"stopped";pl""]
      else wh  /* whathappened */
]

/* Read a file into pr

gi                          /* progin */
[
   int k
   k=1
   while((k=k+1)<7) [
      if(ln(k)==0) [
         while((k=k+1)<7) ln(k)=' '
      ]
   ]
   pn k=readfile(ln+3,pr+pe+1,pr+lp,1)
   pl ""
   if(k<0)return
   pe=pe+k
   la=countch(pr+1,pr+pe,10)
   fa
]

/* Writes all of pr to a file

gu                          /* progout */
[
   int k
   fa
   k=1
   while((k=k+1)<7) [
      if(ln(k)==0) [
```

```
        while((k=k+1)<7) ln(k)=' '
      ]
    ]
    pn writefile(ln+3,pr+1,pr+pe,1)
    pl""
]
```

Appendix F

The tiny-c Interpreter Files

The tiny-c interpreter is divided into eleven source code files on the tiny-c diskette. Two of these files, TC.H and GLDECL.H, are header files and are included in each of the other files when they are compiled. The remaining nine files, MAIN.C, ANALYZE.C, ENTER.C, SCAN.C, STACK.C, SYMBOL.C, UTILITY.C, MC.C, and CUSTOM.C contain the C functions described in Chapter 4. This appendix consists of a listing of each of these files.

TC.H

```
/*
**  tiny-c Interpreter Header File
*/

/*
**  tiny-c error codes
*/
#define STATERR          1
#define CURSERR          2
#define SYMBOLERR        3
#define RPARENERR        5
#define RANGERR          6
#define CLASSERR         7
#define SYNTAXERR        9
#define LVALERR         14
#define POPERR          15
#define PUSHERR         16
```

```
#define TMFUNERR        17
#define TMVARERR        18
#define TMVALERR        19
#define LINKERR         20
#define ARGSERR         21
#define LBRACERR        22
#define MCERR           24
#define DECLARERR       26
#define KILL            99

/*
**  tiny-c conventions
*/
#define YES              1
#define TRUE             1
#define NO               0
#define FALSE            0
#define NULL             0
#define EOF            (-1)
#define ERR            (-1)
```

```
/*
**  tiny-c sizing constants
*/
#define MAXSTACK        30
#define MAXVAR         200
#define MAXFUN          30
#define MAXPR        20000
#define VLEN             8

/*
**  tiny-c table constants
*/
#define ACTUAL   'A'
#define LVALUE   'L'
#define FNREF    'E'
#define BYTE      1
#define WORD      2

/*
**  tiny-c tokens
*/
#define INTCON    1
#define STRCON    2
#define CHRCON    3

/*
**  tiny-c pseudo storage classes
*/
#define FAST     register
#define GLOBAL   extern
#define LOCAL    static

/*
**  tiny-c pseudo data types
*/
typedef char TEXT, TINY;
typedef int BOOL, COUNT, VOID;
typedef unsigned BYTES;

typedef union datum {
        int     ival;
        TEXT    *dptr;
} DATUM;

typedef struct item {
        TINY    class;
        TINY    lvalue;
        TINY    size;
        DATUM   value;

} ITEM;

typedef struct variable {
        TEXT    vname[VLEN];
        TINY    vclass;
        TINY    vsize;
        COUNT   vlen;
        TEXT    *vptr;
} VARIABLE;
```

```
typedef struct function {
        VARIABLE        *fvar;
        VARIABLE        *lvar;
        VARIABLE        *cache;
        TEXT            *backup;
} FUNCTION;

/*
**  tiny-c macros
*/
#define FOREVER      for (;;)
#define alpha(c)     ('a'<=(c)&&(c)<='z'||'A'<=(c)&&(c)<='Z'||(c)=='_')
#define alphanum(c)  (alpha(c)||'0'<=(c)&&(c)<='9')
#define num(c)       (('0'<=(c)&&(c)<='9')?(c)-'0': -1)

/*
**  machine dependencies
*/
#define BYTEBITS          8
#define BYTEMASK       0377

/*
**  file system interface
*/
typedef int FILE;

#define stdin       0
#define stdout      1
#define stderr      2
```

GLDECL.H

```
/*
** tiny-c Interpreter Global Data Declarations
*/

TEXT *pr, *cursor, *fname, *lname, *errat, *progend, *prused,
     *skip(), *rem();
BOOL leave, brake;
COUNT err, applvl;
ITEM *stackb, *top;
VARIABLE *varb, *nxtvar, *addrval();
FUNCTION *funb, *curfun, *curglobal;
```

MAIN.C

```
/*
** tiny-c Interpreter Main Program
*/

#include "tc.h"
#include "gldecl.h"

VOID main(argc, argv)
COUNT argc;
TEXT *argv[];
{
```

```
        TEXT *version     = "tiny-c/PC Interpreter  Version PC-01-01";
        TEXT *copyright   = "Copyright (c) 1984 by Scott B. Guthery";

        /* Initialize TEXT variables */
        pr = calloc(MAXPR+2, sizeof TEXT);
        cursor = progend = prused = pr;
        fname = lname = errat = NULL;

        /* Initialize BOOLEAN variables */
        leave = brake = NO;

        /* Initialize COUNT variables */
        err = applvl = 0;

        /* Initialize ITEM variables */
        stackb = calloc(MAXSTACK+1, sizeof ITEM);
        top = stackb -1;

        /* Initialize VARIABLE variables */
        varb = calloc(MAXVAR+1, sizeof VARIABLE);
        nxtvar = varb;

        /* Initialize FUNCTION variables */
        funb = calloc(MAXFUN+1, sizeof FUNCTION);
        curfun    = funb - 1;
        curglobal = funb + 1;

        /* Load a tiny-c system program */
        if (((argc <= 1) ? ipl("tinyc.ipl") : ipl(argv[argc-1])) < 0)
            return;

        prused = progend;    /* set the top of the program buffer */
        cursor = pr;
        link();              /* link the system library & the Shell */
        newfun();            /* allocate the 1st local symbol table */
        cursor = pr;
        st();                /* hit the boot button */
}
```

ANALYZE.C

```
/*
** tiny-c Interpreter Statement Analyzer Routines
*/

#include "tc.h"
#include "gldecl.h"

/*
** Match a relational expression optionally followed by an assignment
*/
VOID asgn()
{
        reln();
        /* if there's an = sign, perform an assignment */
        if(lit("=")) eq(asgn());
}
```

```
/*
** Evaluate an arithmetic series:
**      +- term +- term ... +- term
*/
VOID expr()
{
        int ival;

        /* the leading operator, if any, is unary */
        if (lit("-")) {
                term();
                /* negative of term to stack */
                pushint(-toptoi());
        }
        else {
                lit("+");
                /* term to stack */
                term();
        }

        FOREVER {
                if (lit("+")) {
                        term();
                        /* sum of top values */
                        pushint(toptoi() + toptoi());
                }
                else if (lit("-")) {
                        term();
                        ival = toptoi();
                        /* difference of top values */
                        pushint(toptoi() - ival);
                }
                else return;
        }
}

/*
** Evaluate a factor:
**       i) ( asgn )
**      ii) constant
**     iii) variable or function reference
*/
VOID factor ()
{
    int contype, index;
    DATUM value;
    VARIABLE *vbl;

    /* if you see a (, it's a ( asgn ) */
    if (lit("(")) {
        asgn();
        if (!lit(")"))
            error(RPARENERR);
    }
    /* if you can match a constant, that's what it is */
        else if (contype = const()) {
            switch(contype) {
            case INTCON: /* integer constant */
                pushint(atoi(fname));
```

```
            break;
        case STRCON: /* string constant */
            value.dptr = fname;
            push(1, ACTUAL, BYTE, &value);
            break;
        case CHRCON: /* character constant */
            value.ival = *fname;
            push(0, ACTUAL, BYTE, &value);
            break;
        }
}
/* otherwise, it better be a known symbol */
else if (symname()) {

    /* if it's MC, call it */
    if (*fname == 'M' && *lname == 'C')
            enter(NULL);
    /* otherwise, look it up in the symbol table */
    else if (vbl = addrval()) {

        /* if it's not a function reference, it's a variable reference */
        if (vbl->vclass != FNREF) {
            /* a ( means it's an array reference */
            if (lit("(")) {
                if (vbl->vclass == 0)
                        return error(CLASSERR);
                /* compute the subscript */
                asgn();
                if (!lit(")"))
                        return error(RPARENERR);
                index = toptoi();
                /* make sure it's in range */
                if (vbl->vlen > 1 && (index < 0 || index >= vbl->vlen))
                        return error(RANGERR);
                /* compute the offset */
                value.dptr = vbl->vptr + index * vbl->vsize;
                    /* and push the value */
                    push(vbl->vclass-1, LVALUE, vbl->vsize, &value);
                }
                /* otherwise it's an plain variable */
                else {
                    /* get the address */
                    if (vbl->vclass == 0) value.dptr = vbl->vptr;
                    /* force an indirection for
                       unsubscripted array references */
                    else value.dptr = &vbl->vptr;
                    /* and push the value */
                    push(vbl->vclass, LVALUE, vbl->vsize, &value);
                }
            }
            /* if it's a function reference, call it */
            else enter(vbl->vptr);
        }
        else error(SYMBOLERR);
    }
    else error(SYNTAXERR);
}

/*
```

```
** Evaluate an expression or a comparison of expressions
*/
VOID reln()
{
        int left;

        expr();   /* match the expression */

        /* look for a relational operator & apply it if found */
        if (lit("==")) {
                left = toptoi();
                expr();
                pushint(left == toptoi());
        }
        else if (lit("!=")) {
                left = toptoi();
                expr();
                pushint(left != toptoi());
        }
        else if (lit("<=")) {
                left = toptoi();
                expr();
                pushint(left <= toptoi());
        }
        else if (lit(">=")) {
                left = toptoi();
                expr();
                pushint(left >= toptoi());
        }
        else if (lit(">")) {
                left = toptoi();
                expr();
                pushint(left > toptoi());
        }
        else if (lit("<")) {
                left = toptoi();
                expr();
                pushint(left < toptoi());
        }
}

/*
** Skip a statement
*/
VOID skipst()
{
        FAST TEXT *c;

        /* bypass a leading remark */
        rem();

        /* skip a compound statement */
        if (lit("["))
                skip('[',']');

        /* skip an 'if' statement */
        else if (lit("if")) {
                lit("(");
                skip('(',')');
```

```
                skipst();
                if (lit("else"))
                        skipst();
        }

        /* skip a 'while' statement */
        else if (lit("while")) {
                lit("(");
                skip('(',')');
                skipst();
        }

        /* skip a one-liner */
        else {
                c = cursor;
                while(*c != ';' && *c != ']' &&
                      *c != '\n' && c <= progend) c++;
                if (c > progend)
                        return error(CURSERR);
                cursor = c + 1;
        }

        /* bypass a trailing remark */
        rem();
}

/*
** Evaluate a statement
*/
VOID st()
{
        TEXT *repeat, *body;

        /* if the error light is lit, don't bother */
        if(err) return;

        /* bypass a leading remark */
        rem();

        /* handle any beginning-of-statement business */
        stbegin();

        /* parse a 'char' statement */
        if (lit("char")) {
                valloc('C', NULL);
                while(lit(","))
                        valloc('C', NULL);
                lit(";");
        }

        /* parse an 'int' statement */
        else if (lit("int")) {
                valloc('I', NULL);
                while(lit(","))
                        valloc('I', NULL);
                lit(";");
        }

        /* parse a compound statement */
        else if (lit("[")) {
```

```
        while(!leave && !brake && !lit("]") && !err)
                st();
}

/* parse an 'if' statement */
else if (lit("if")) {
        lit("("); asgn(); lit(")");
        if (toptoi()) {
                st();
                if (lit("else"))
                        skipst();
        }
        else {
                skipst();
                if (lit("else"))
                        st();
        }
}

/* parse a 'while' statement */
else if (lit("while")) {
        repeat = cursor;
        FOREVER {
        lit("("); asgn(); lit(")");
        if (toptoi()) {
                body = cursor;
                        st();
                        if (!leave && !brake && !err) {
                                cursor = repeat;
                                continue;
                        }
                        else {
                                skipst(cursor = body);
                                if(brake) brake = NO;
                                break;
                        }
                }
                else {
                        skipst();
                        break;
                }
                }
        }

        /* parse a null statement */
        else if (lit(";")) {
                ;
        }

        /* parse a 'return' statement */
        else if (lit("return")) {
                if (lit(";") || lit("\n")) pushint(0);
                else asgn();
                leave = YES;
        }

        /* parse a 'break' statement */
        else if (lit("break")) {
```

```
                brake = YES;
        }

        /* parse an expression statement */
        else {
                asgn();
                toptoi();
        }

        /* bypass optional semicolon and trailing remarks */
        lit(";");
        rem();
}

/*
** Evaluate a multiplicative series:
**      factor *%/ factor ... *%/ factor
*/
VOID term()
{
        int ival;

        factor();
        FOREVER {
                if (lit("*")) {
                        ival = toptoi(); factor();
                        /* product of top values */
                        pushint(ival * toptoi());
                }
                else if (*cursor == '/' && *(cursor+1) != '*') {
                        cursor++; /* careful of comments */
                        ival = toptoi(); factor();
                        /* quotient of top values */
                        pushint(ival / toptoi());
                }
                else if (lit("%")) {
                        ival = toptoi(); factor();
                        /* remainder of top values */
                        pushint(ival % toptoi());
                }
                else return;
        }
}

/*
** Parse an element of a 'char' or 'int' declaration list
*/
VOID valloc(type, passed)
TINY type;
TINY *passed;
{
        TEXT *fnsave, *lnsave;
        static VARIABLE vbl;

        /* get it's name */
        if (symname()) {

                vbl.vclass = 0;
```

```
		/* compute it's length */
		if (lit("(")) {
			fnsave = fname; lnsave = lname;
			vbl.vclass = 1;
			/* compute the dimension */
			asgn();
			fname = fnsave; lname = lnsave;
			lit(")");
			vbl.vlen = toptoi() + 1;
		}
		else vbl.vlen = 1;

		vbl.vsize = (type == 'C') ? BYTE : WORD;

		vbl.vptr = passed;

		/* add it to the symbol table */
		newvar(&vbl);
	}
	else error(SYMBOLERR);
}
```

ENTER.C

```
/*
** tiny-c Interpreter Calling & Linking Routines
*/

#include "tc.h"
#include "gldecl.h"

/*
** Enter a called function
*/
VOID enter(entry)
TEXT *entry;
{
	TEXT *retern;
	COUNT argc;
	ITEM *arg;

	argc = 0; arg = top + 1;
	lit("(");

	/* if there are any arguments, evaluate 'em and
	   leave their values on the stack */
	if (!lit(")") && *cursor != ']'  && *cursor != ';'
		      && *cursor != '\n' && *cursor !='/') {
		FOREVER {
			asgn();
			argc++;
			if (!lit(",")) break;
		}
		/* if there was trouble, clean up the stack & return */
		if (err) {
			while (argc--) pop();
			pushint(0);
			return;
```

```
		}
		lit(")");
	}

	/* if it's a Machine Call, bug out to the MC routine */
	if (entry == NULL) {
		MC(argc);
		return;
	}

	/* otherwise, it's a call on a tiny-c function */
	retern = cursor;  /* mark where you are */
	cursor = entry;   /* set cursor to where you're going */
	newfun();  /* open up a new local symbol block */

	/* transfer argument values to formal argument variables */
	FOREVER {
		rem();
		if (lit("int")) {
			setarg('I', arg++);
			while (lit(","))
				setarg('I', arg++);
			lit(";");
		}
		else if (lit("char")) {
			setarg('C', arg++);
			while (lit(","))
				setarg('C', arg++);
			lit(";");
		}
		else break;
	}

	/* if the number of argument values is not equal to the
	  number of argument variables, light the error light */
	if (arg != top + 1) error(ARGSERR);

	/* clear the argument values off the stack */
	while(argc--) pop();

	/* if everything is ok, turn the
	   interpreter loose in the function */
	if(!err) st();

	/* if the function didn't return a value, push a zero */
	if(leave == NO) pushint(0);
	/* otherwise, make the top an actual */
	else {
		pushint(toptoi());
		leave = NO;
	}

	/* pop the cursor & restore caller's local symbols */
	cursor = retern;
	fundon();
}

/*
** Allocate externals
```

```
*/
VOID link()
{
        VARIABLE vbl;

        newfun();  /* establish the system global level */
        while (cursor < progend - 1 && !err) {
                rem();

                /* skip external statements */
                if (lit("[")) {
                        skip('[', ']');
                }

                /* allocate an external 'int' list */
                else if (lit("int")) {
                        valloc('I', NULL);
                        while (lit(","))
                                valloc('I', NULL);
                        lit(";");
                }

                /* allocate an external 'char' list */
                else if (lit("char")) {
                        valloc('C', NULL);
                        while (lit(","))
                                valloc('C', NULL);
                        lit(";");
                }

                /* shift from system globals to regular globals */
                else if (lit("endlibrary"))
                        newfun();

                /* allocate a function name */
                else if (symname()) {
                        vbl.vclass = FNREF; vbl.vsize = WORD;
                        vbl.vlen = 1; vbl.vptr = cursor;
                        newvar(&vbl);
                        /* skip over the function's body */
                        while (*cursor != '[' && cursor < progend) cursor++;
                        if (*cursor != '[' ) return error(LBRACERR);
                        else {
                                cursor++;
                                skip('[', ']');
                        }
                }
                else error(LINKERR);
        }
}

/*
** Set formal function argument variables to their called values
*/
VOID setarg(type, arg)
ITEM *arg;
TINY type;
{
        FAST unsigned word;
```

```
	/* if it's an actual, just set it */
	if (arg->lvalue == ACTUAL)
		valloc(type, arg->value.ival);

	/* if it's a byte indirect, the call will make it an 'int' */
	else if (arg->size == BYTE && arg->class == 0)
		valloc(type, *arg->value.dptr);

	/* otherwise, we have to assemble it ourselves */
	else {
		word = *(arg->value.dptr + 1);
		word = (word << BYTEBITS) | (*arg->value.dptr & BYTEMASK);

		valloc(type, word);
	}
}
```

SCAN.C

```
/*
** tiny-c Interpreter Scanning Routines
*/

#include "tc.h"
#include "gldecl.h"

/*
** Skip over blanks & tabs
*/
TEXT *blanks()
{
	FAST TEXT *c = cursor;

	while (*c == ' ' || *c == '\t' || *c == '\r') c++;
	return cursor = c;
}

/*
** Match integer, string, and character constants
*/
COUNT const()
{
	FAST TEXT *c;

	c = blanks();

	/* try for an integer constant */
	if (*c == '+' || *c == '-' || num(*c) != -1) {
		fname = cursor;
		while (num(*c) != -1) c++ ;
		lname = c-1; cursor = c;
		return INTCON;
	}

	/* try for a string */
	else if (*c == '\"') {
		fname = ++c;
		while (*c && *c != '\"' && c++ < progend);
```

```
		if (c <= progend) {
			*c++ = 0; cursor = c; lname = c-2;
			return STRCON;
		}
		else return error(CURSERR);
	}

	/* try for a character constant */
	else if (*c == '\'') {
		fname = ++c;
		while (*c != '\'' && c++ < progend);
		if (c <= progend) {
			cursor = ++c; lname = c-2;
			return CHRCON;
		}
		else return error(CURSERR);
	}

	/* none of the above */
	else return 0;
}

/*
** Match a literal
*/
BOOL lit(s)
FAST TEXT *s;
{
	FAST TEXT *c = cursor;

	if(*c == ' ' || *c == '\t' || *c == '\r') c = blanks();
	if(*c++ != *s++) return NO;
	while (*s)
		if (*c++ != *s++) return NO;
	cursor = c;
	return YES;
}

/*
** Skip over remarks and adjacent white space
*/
TEXT *rem()
{
	FAST TEXT *c;

	while((c = blanks()) <= progend) {
		if (*c == '\n'|| *c == '\r') c++;
		else if (*c != '/' || *(c + 1) != '*')
			return cursor = c;
		else while (*c++ != '\n' && c <= progend);
		cursor = c;
	}
	return progend;
}

/*
** Skip balanced delimiters and everyting inbetween
*/
TEXT *skip(left, right)
```

```
char left, right;
{
        FAST TEXT *c;
        FAST COUNT parity;

        parity = 1;
        for (c = cursor; c <= progend; c++) {
                if (*c == left) parity++;
                else if (*c == right) parity--;
                if (parity == 0)
                        return cursor = ++c;
        }
        return error(CURSERR);
}

/*
** Match a symbol name and set fname & lname
*/
BOOL symname()
{
        FAST TEXT *c;

        c = blanks();
        if (!alpha(*c)) return NO;
        fname = c++;
        while (alphanum(*c)) c++;
        lname = c-1; cursor = c;
        return YES;
}
```

STACK.C

```
/*
** tiny-c Interpreter Stack Routines
*/

#include "tc.h"
#include "gldecl.h"

/*
** Perform an assignment
*/
VOID eq()
{

        int ival;

        ival = toptoi();
        /* make sure you've got an lvalue */
        if (top->lvalue == LVALUE) {
                if (top->class == 0)
                        movn(top->value.dptr, &ival, top->size);
                else
                        movn(top->value.dptr, &ival, WORD);
                pop();
                /* assignments have values too */
                pushint(ival);
```

```
	}
	else error(LVALERR);
}

/*
** Pop the tiny-c stack & return the ival
*/
int pop()
{
	if (top >= stackb) return (top--)->value.ival;
	else return error(POPERR);
}

/*
** Push item parts onto the tiny-c stack
*/
VOID push(pclass, plvalue, psize, pdatum)
TINY pclass, plvalue, psize;
DATUM *pdatum;
{
	if (++top <= stackb + MAXSTACK) {
		top->class = pclass;
		top->lvalue = plvalue;
		top->size = psize;
		if (pclass == ACTUAL && plvalue == 0)
			top->value.ival = pdatum->ival;
		else top->value.dptr = pdatum->dptr;
	}
	else error(PUSHERR);
}

/*
** Push an integer onto the tiny-c stack
*/
VOID pushint(ival)
int ival;
{
	if (++top <= stackb + MAXSTACK) {
		top->class = 0;
		top->lvalue = ACTUAL;
		top->size = WORD;
		top->value.ival = ival;
	}
	else error(PUSHERR);
}

/*
** Resolve the item on the top of the stack & return it
*/
int toptoi()
{


	FAST int topval;

	/* if it's an actual, just pop it */
	if (top->lvalue == ACTUAL)
		return pop();

	/* if it's a byte indirect, sign extend it */
```

```
        else if (top->size == BYTE && top->class == 0)
                topval = *top->value.dptr;

        /* otherwise, assemble it */
        else {
                topval = *(top->value.dptr + 1);
                topval = (topval << BYTEBITS) |
                         (*top->value.dptr & BYTEMASK);
        }
        pop();
        return topval;
}
```

SYMBOL.C

```
/*
** tiny-c Interpreter Symbol Table Routines
*/

#include "tc.h"
#include "gldecl.h"

/*
** Search 1) current locals
**        2) application globals
** and    3) system globals
** for a symbol name.
*/
VARIABLE *addrval()
{
        TEXT name[VLEN];
        FAST FUNCTION *sfun;
        FAST VARIABLE *pvar;

        canon(name);
        for (sfun = curfun; ; sfun = (sfun == curfun) ? curglobal : funb) {
                /* maybe we just used it ... check the cache */
                if(!strcmp(name, sfun->cache->vname, VLEN))
                        return(sfun->cache);
                /* no soap ... hunt the symbol */
                for (pvar = sfun->fvar; pvar <= sfun->lvar; pvar++)
                        if (!strncmp(name, pvar->vname, VLEN))
                                return(sfun->cache = pvar);
                if (sfun == funb) break;
        }
        error(DECLARERR);
        return NULL;
}

/*
** Canonicalize the symbol between fname & lname
*/
VOID canon(name)
FAST TEXT *name;
{
        FAST COUNT i;
```

```
        for (i = VLEN; i > 0 && fname <= lname; i--)
                *name++ = *fname++;
        if(i == 0) *(name-1) = *lname;
        else *name = '\0';
}

/*
** Pop function stack ... return to previous local symbol table
*/
VOID fundon()
{
        nxtvar = curfun->fvar;
        prused = (curfun--)->backup;
}

/*
** Open up a new local symbol table
*/
VOID newfun()
{
        static VARIABLE nullvar = {NULL, NULL, NULL, NULL, NULL};

        if(++curfun <= funb + MAXFUN) {
                curfun->fvar   = nxtvar;
                curfun->lvar   = nxtvar - 1;
                curfun->cache  = &nullvar;
                curfun->backup = prused;
        }
        else error(TMFUNERR);
}

/*
** Push a new variable on the variable stack
*/
VOID newvar(vbl)
FAST VARIABLE *vbl;
{
        static char *c;

        if (nxtvar <= varb + MAXVAR) {
                canon(nxtvar->vname);
                nxtvar->vclass = vbl->vclass;
                nxtvar->vsize = vbl->vsize;
                nxtvar->vlen = vbl->vlen;
                /* if it's indirect, just pass the pointer */
                if (vbl->vptr != 0 && vbl->vclass != 0)
                        nxtvar->vptr = vbl->vptr;

                /* otherwise, allocate some new room */
                else {  int nbytes = vbl->vsize * vbl->vlen;
                        nxtvar->vptr = prused + 1;
                        if ( prused + nbytes <= pr + MAXPR) {
                             prused += nbytes;

                /* if it's being passed, move the value */
                if (vbl->vptr)
                    movn(nxtvar->vptr, &vbl->vptr, vbl->vsize);
                /* otherwise, zero out the new space */
                else
```

```
                                        _setmem(nxtvar->vptr, nbytes, '\0');
                                }
                                  else error(TMVALERR);
                        }

                        /* expand the current local symbol table */
                        curfun->lvar = nxtvar++;
                }
                else error(TMVARERR);
}
```

UTILITY.C

```
/*
** tiny-c Interpreter Utility Functions
*/

#include "tc.h"
#include "gldecl.h"

/*
** Set the error flags
*/
VOID error(number)
int number;
{
        if (!err) {
                err = number;
                errat = cursor;
        }
        return(NULL);
}

/*
** Handle an MC error
**   - pop the args
**   - set the MCERR error flag
*/
VOID mcerror(args)
int args;
{
        int i;

        for(i = 0; i < args; i++) pop();
        return(pushint(error(MCERR)));
}

/*
** Move n bytes from b to a without regard for overlap
*/
VOID movn(a, b, n)
FAST TEXT *a, *b;
FAST COUNT n;
{
        /* while(n-- > 0) *a++ = *b++; */
        /* For speed sake, use the DeSmet C library move */
```

```
        _move(n, b, a);
}

/*
** Wait ticks 10ths of a second.
*/
GLOBAL unsigned _rax, _rds, _rdx;

VOID wait(ticks)
int ticks;
{
        FAST int tick_end;

        _rax=0;_rds=-1;
        _doint(0x1A);
        tick_end = _rdx + ticks;
        while(_rdx < tick_end)
            _doint(0x1A);
}
```

MC.C

```
/*
** tiny-c Interpreter Machine Calls (MC) for the IBM PC & IBM PCjr
*/

#include "tc.h"
#include "gldecl.h"

#define PUTC         1
#define GETC         2
#define OPEN         3
#define READ         4
#define WRITE        5
#define CLOSE        6
#define MOVEBL       7
#define COUNTCH      8
#define SCANN        9
#define HALT        10
#define APPL        11
#define CHRDY       12
#define PUTBL       13
#define PUTN        14
#define GETLN       15
#define SETMEM      16
#define BEEP        17
#define checkargs(n)  if(args!=n)return(mcerror(args))

unsigned _rax, _rbx, _rcx, _rdx,  _rsi, _rdi, _res, _rds;

#define _8253_Timer_2        (0x42)
#define _8253_Control        (0x43)
#define _8255_Port_B         (0x61)

VOID MC(args)
int args;
{
```

```
int i;
char *c;
static FILE file[10];

args--;
if((i = pop()) >= 1000)
    usermc(args, i-1000);
else switch(i) {

case PUTC:
        checkargs(1);
        c = toptoi();
        return(pushint(co(c?c:'"')));

case GETC:
        checkargs(0);
        co(c = ci());
        return(push(0, 'A', 1, &c));

case OPEN: { int unit, size, mode; char *name;
        checkargs(4);
        unit = toptoi();
        size = toptoi();
        name = toptoi();
        mode = toptoi();
        file[unit] = fopen(name, (mode==2)?"w":"r");
        return(pushint(file[unit]?0:-1));
}

case READ: { int unit, nbytes; char *buffer;
        checkargs(2);
        unit = toptoi(); buffer = toptoi();
        nbytes = fread(buffer, 1, 512, file[unit]);
        return(pushint(nbytes?nbytes:-1));
}

case WRITE: { int unit; char *from, *to;
        checkargs(3);
        unit = toptoi(); to = toptoi(); from = toptoi();
        return(pushint(fwrite(from, 1, to-from+1, file[unit])));
}

case CLOSE:
        checkargs(1);
        return(pushint(fclose(file[toptoi()])));

case MOVEBL: { char *start, *end; int offset;
        checkargs(3);
        offset = toptoi(); end = toptoi(); start = toptoi();
        return(pushint(_move(end-start+1, start, start+offset)));
}

case COUNTCH: { char *from, *to; int ch;
        checkargs(3);
        ch = toptoi(); to = toptoi(); from = toptoi();
        for(i = 0, c = from; c <= to; c++)
                i += (*c == ch);
        return(pushint(i));
}
```

```
case SCANN: { char *from, *to; int ch, *nptr, last = -1;
        checkargs(4);
        nptr = toptoi(); ch = toptoi();
        to = toptoi(); from = toptoi();
        for(c = from; *nptr > 0 && c <= to; c++, last++)
                if(*c == ch) (*nptr)--;
        return(pushint(last));
}

case HALT:
        exit();


case APPL:
   { int save[10];
        checkargs(4);
        save[0] = cursor;
        save[1] = progend;
        save[2] = prused;
        save[3] = curglobal;
        save[4] = cursor = toptoi();
        prused = progend = toptoi();
        link();
        curglobal = curfun;
        cursor = toptoi();
        newfun();
        save[5] = toptoi();
        save[6] = top;
        if(!err) {
                appl vl++;
                prdone(st(prbegin()));
                appl vl--;
        }
        fundon();fundon();
        save[7] = cursor - save[4];
        if(err)
                save[7] = errat - save[4];
        movn(save[5]+2, &save[7], 2);
        movn(save[5],   &err, 2);
        cursor    = save[0];
        progend   = save[1];
        prused    = save[2];
        curglobal = save[3];
        top       = save[6];
        err = 0;
        return(pushint(0));
}

case CHRDY:
        checkargs(0);
        return(pushint(csts()));


case PUTBL: { FAST char *s, *from, *to;
        checkargs(2);
        to = toptoi(); from = toptoi();
        for(s = from; s<= to; s++)
                putchar(*s?*s:'"');
        return(pushint(0));
}
```

```
case PUTN:
        checkargs(1);
        return(pushint(printf("%d", toptoi())));

case GETLN:
        checkargs(1);
        c = toptoi();
        gets(c);
        return(pushint(strlen(c)));

case SETMEM: { int ch, n; char *start;
        checkargs(3);
        ch = toptoi(); n = toptoi(); start = toptoi();
        return(pushint(_setmem(start, n, ch)));
}

case BEEP: { int frequency, duration; char port_value;

        checkargs(2);
        duration  = toptoi();
        frequency = (frequency = toptoi()) > 0 ?
                     1190000/frequency : 0 ;

        /* Tell the 8353 what's comin' */
        _outb(0xB6, _8253_Control);

        /* Place the frequency in Timer 2 of the 8253 */
        _outb((char)frequency,        _8253_Timer_2);
        _outb((char)(frequency>>8), _8253_Timer_2);

        /* Start Timer 2 and attach its output to the speaker */
        port_value = _inb(_8255_Port_B);
        _outb((port_value | 0x03) & 0x9F, _8255_Port_B);

        /* Wait 'duration' ticks */
        wait(duration);

        /* Reset the speaker */
                _outb(port_value, _8255_Port_B);

                return(pushint(0));
        }

        default: return(mcerror(args));
        }
}
```

CUSTOM.C

```
/*
** tiny-c Interpreter Customizing Routines
*/

#include "tc.h"
#include "gldecl.h"

#define ESC 27
```

```
/*
** This stbegin() checks for application program interrupt which is
** defined to be the mashing of the Esc key.
*/
VOID stbegin(){
        int c;

        if(applvl && (c = csts()) && (c == ESC)) {
                error(KILL);
                ci();
        }
}

/*
** Do nothing at the entry to an application program
*/
VOID prbegin(){}

/*
** Do nothing at the exit of an application program
*/
VOID prdone(){}

/*
** Initial Program Load the pr array
**    - translate from non-tiny-c editor to tiny-c format if necessary
*/
VOID ipl(file)
char  *file;
{
        FILE iop;
        register int c;

        if(!(iop = fopen(file, "r"))) {
                printf("Can't open IPL file %s\n", file);
                exit();
        }

        /* Squeeze out the carriage returns and the nulls */
        while((c = getc(iop)) != EOF)
                if(c != '\r' && c != '\0') *cursor++ = c;
        progend = --cursor;
        return(0);
}

/*
** User Machine Calls
**     - MC(a, ..., MC_number) with MC_number >= 1000.
**     - 1000 is subtracted from MC_number before usermc is called by MC.
**     - these user MC calls are for the sound system of the IBM PCjr
*/

#define NOISE       0
#define SOUND       1
#define WARBLE      2

#define checkargs(n)     if(args!=n)return(mcerror(args));

#define _8253_Timer_2     (0X42)
```

```
#define _8253_Control       (0X43)
#define _8255_Port_B        (0X61)
#define _76496_Control      (0XC0)

unsigned _rax, _rbx, _rcx, _rdx, _rsi, _rdi, _res, _rds;

VOID usermc(args, MC_number)
int args, MC_number;
{
        switch(MC_number) {

        case NOISE: { char noise, attenuation;
        checkargs(2);
        attenuation = 15-toptoi();
        noise = toptoi();
         /* Attach the speaker to the 76496 */
        _outb(_inb(_8255_Port_B) | 0x60, _8255_Port_B);
         /* Program the noise generator of the 76496 */
        _outb(attenuation | 0xF0, _76496_Control);
        _outb(noise | 0xE0, _76496_Control);
         return(pushint(0));
         }

        case SOUND: { char voice, attenuation, byte; int frequency;
        checkargs(3);
        attenuation = 15-toptoi();
        frequency = (frequency = toptoi()) > 0 ? 111844/frequency : 0 ;
        voice = ((voice = toptoi()) < 0 ? 0 : (voice > 2) ? 2 : voice) << 5;
         /* Attach the speaker to the 76496 */
        _outb(_inb(_8255_Port_B) | 0x60, _8255_Port_B);
         /* Program the tone generator of the 76496 */
        _outb( 0x80 | voice | (frequency & 0x000F), _76496_Control);
        _outb((frequency >> 4) & 0x3F, _76496_Control);
        _outb( 0x90 | voice | attenuation, _76496_Control);
         return(pushint(0));
         }

       case WARBLE: {int frequency;
        checkargs(1);
        frequency = (frequency = toptoi()) > 0 ? 111844/frequency : 0 ;
         /* Send the argument to the latched register of the 76496 */
        _outb((frequency >> 4) & 0x3F, _76496_Control);
         return(pushint(0));
         }

       default: return(mcerror(args));
       }
```

Bibliography

Aho, Alfred, and Ullman, Jeffrey. *Principles of Compiler Design*. Reading, Mass.: Addison-Wesley, 1978.

Brown, Peter. *Writing Interactive Compilers and Interpreters*. New York: John Wiley and Sons, 1979.

BYTE Special Issue on The C Language. August 1983.

Feurzeig, Wally, et al. "Programming Languages as a Conceptual Framework for Teaching Mathematics." *BBN Report* No. 2165, June 1971.

Duncan, Ray. "tiny-c Interpreter on CDOS." *Dr. Dobb's Journal*. May 1979.

Gibson, Tom. "Caution: Structured Programming Can Be Habit-Forming." *Creative Computing*, January 1979.

Gibson, Tom, and Guthery, Scott. "Structured Programming, C and tiny-c." *Dr. Dobb's Journal,* May 1980.

Gilbreath, Jim. "A High-Level Language Benchmark." *BYTE,* September 1981.

Gries, David. "On Structured Programming—A Reply to Smoliar." *CACM,* November 1974.

Hancock, Les. "Growing, Pruning and Climbing Binary Trees with tiny-c." *Dr. Dobb's Journal,* June/July 1979.

Hancock, Les, and Krieger, Morris. *The C Primer*. New York: McGraw-Hill, 1983.

Hughes, Phillip. "BASIC, Pascal or tiny-c." *BYTE,* October 1981.

Kemeny, J.G., and Kurtz, T.E. *BASIC Programming*. New York: John Wiley and Sons, 1967.

Kern, Christopher. "A User's Look at tiny-c." *Byte,* December 1979.

Kernighan, Brian, and Plauger, P. J. *Software Tools.* Addison-Wesley, 1967.

Kernighan, Brian, and Ritchie, Dennis. The C Programming Language. Englewood Cliffs, N.J.: Prentice-Hall, 1978.

Kernighan, Brian, and Pike, Rob. The UNIX Programming Environment. Englewood Cliffs, N.J.: Prentice-Hall, 1984.

Madden, J. Gregory, "C: A Language for Microprocessors?" *BYTE*, October 1977.

McIntire, Thomas. *Software Interpreters for Microcomputers*. New York: John Wiley and Sons, 1978.

Ritchie, Dennis and Thompson, Ken. "The UNIX Time-Sharing System." *CACM*, March 1974.

Ritchie, Dennis, et al. "The C Programming Language." Murray Hill, N.J.: Bell Telephone Laboratories, October 1975.

Ritchie, Dennis; Johnson, Steve; Lesk, Michael; and Kernighan, Brian. "The C Programming Language." *Dr. Dobbs Journal*, May 1980.

Sargent, Murray, and Shoemaker, Richard. *The IBM Personal Computer from the Inside Out*. Reading, Mass.: Addison-Wesley, 1984.

Snyder, Alan. "A Portable Compiler for the Language C." *MIT Project MAC Technical Report 149*, May 1975.

Wexelblat, Richard. "The Consequences of One's First Programming Language." *Software - Practice and Experience*, Vol. II, 1980.

Zahn, Carl. *Notes: A Guide to the C Programming Language*. New York: Yourdon Press, 1979.

Index

Edited by Stephen Moore